TANK SPOTTER'S GUIDE

METRO BOOKS
New York

TANK SPOTTER'S GUIDE

Compiled by Marcus Cowper and Christopher Pannell

Introduction by David Fletcher of The Tank Museum

METRO BOOKS
New York

An Imprint of Sterling Publishing
387 Park Avenue South
New York, NY 10016

CONVERSION TABLE

1 inch: 2.54cm	1 foot: 0.31m
1 yard: 0.91m	1 mile: 1.61km
1 millimetre (mm): 0.04 in	1 centimetre (cm): 0.40 in
1 metre (m): 1.09 yards	1 kilometre (km): 0.62 miles
	1 kilogram (kg): 2.21 lb

CONTENTS

INTRODUCTION

Nearly one hundred years ago, on 15 September 1916, fighting tanks went into battle for the very first time and added a new dimension to warfare. Those first tanks were British but they were soon followed by French, German and American tanks so that by 1918, when World War I ended, tanks formed a significant part of most of the combatant armies.

Tanks have changed over the last 100 years, mostly they have grown bigger and heavier with thicker armour plate and massive guns so they need much more powerful engines to move them along, more fuel to power the engine and an ever greater reliance on technology.

Today the tank is in service virtually all around the world and although it has changed shape dramatically compared with those lumbering monsters of 1916, the modern tank still embodies the three main characteristics of all tanks; that is Firepower, Mobility and Protection.

Firepower of course means guns, but not just guns; it includes sights and rangefinders from the crude early telescopes to the laser rangefinders used today.

Mobility is self-explanatory although it includes such things as tracks, suspension and steering systems which are peculiar to track laying vehicles.

Protection in its normal sense means armour but it can also be taken to include speed, height, camouflage, smoke screens and even the use of ground to hide or protect a tank.

Tank spotting is not difficult, they are big, noisy things but it is a lot harder to identify them, to learn to tell one type from another and know which nationality it is. Which is why a book such as this is so useful as a beginner's guide. Learn the shapes, count the wheels and study the guns. They are all different and once you have become familiar with the tanks shown here visit a museum and look at the real thing.

Here at the Tank Museum in the United Kingdom we have one of the finest collections of tanks in the world. You can walk right up to them, touch them if you like and take photographs. Our website www.tankmuseum.org takes you further into this fascinating subject and that is only the start. There are books on tanks, audio visual presentations and all shapes and sizes of models if you want to set up your own Tank Museum in miniature.

Even so there is one thing that we should never forget – the crew. Most tanks these days require four or five people to drive, load the guns, fire the guns, work the communications equipment and, of course, take command. Back in World War I most tanks required as many as eight men to make everything work and this in the most appalling conditions. But despite many improvements the crew of a tank of today are still the same as they ever were. They form a tightly knit team, professional, dedicated, highly trained and incredibly brave.

Study the tanks in this book, learn to recognize them and find out how they work, but above all remember that they are nothing without the people inside them. We don't have many remote control tanks yet so every time you see a tank roaring along, at a military show or on television, think of the crew, cooped up inside who have to control it and, maybe, take it into battle.

David Fletcher
The Tank Museum

THE MARK I

The Mark I tank had its combat debut on 15 September 1916 near the villages of Flers and Courcelette villages, part of the Somme battlefield. Their performance was mixed, with many of the 32 tanks committed to combat falling foul of shell holes or mechanical problems. However, the few that broke through the enemy lines caused considerable damage. This minor engagement was the start of the development of tanks and armoured warfare that so dominated the battlefields of the 20th century.

The origins of the British Mark I tank lie in the Landship Committee set up by Winston Churchill, First Lord of the Admiralty, in February 1915. This led to the development of a prototype tracked vehicle, the No. 1 Lincoln Machine that was later modified into *Little Willie*, which proved that the tracked concept worked. A full-size prototype was built, variously known as 'His Majesty's Land Ship Centipede', 'Big Willie' and 'Mother'. This was demonstrated before numerous dignitaries and accepted for service, with 100 vehicles being ordered. Responsibility for the project transferred to the War Office and the Ministry of Munitions, and the new vehicle was codenamed the 'tank'.

The new machine was split into two different types: the 'male', which was equipped with the long, 40-caliber, 6-pdr gun, and the 'female', which mounted only machine guns. The Mark I was just armoured enough to withstand small-arms fire and shell splinters. Four men were required to drive the tank: the commander, driver and two gearsmen.

50 of the new tanks were organized into two companies of the Heavy Section, Machine Gun Corps, each 25 strong, and shipped to France where they took part in the closing days of the Somme campaign. Their impact was such that British Commander-in-Chief General Douglas Haig ordered 1,000 more tanks for service. Mark I tanks were also used in the Middle East, with eight tanks being shipped to the Egyptian Expeditionary Force in time for the battles around Gaza. Mark Is saw further action on the Western Front at the battles of Messines and Arras, but by this time they were being replaced by the Mark IIs.

HIS MAJESTY'S LAND SHIP *CENTIPEDE*;

otherwise *Big Willie* or *Mother*

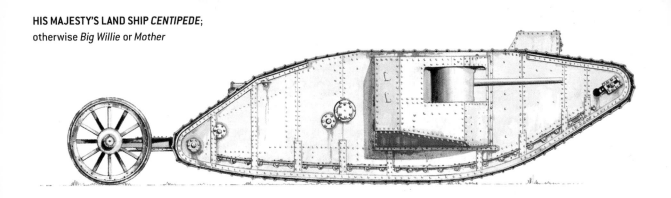

SPECIFICATIONS

Crew: 8

Weight: 28.5 tonnes (31.4 tons)

Power-to-weight ratio: 3.7bhp/ton

Overall length: 9.9m (32.5ft)

Overall width: 4.2m (13.8ft)

Overall height: 2.4m (7.9ft)

Ground pressure: 12.6kg/74.8cm²

Engine: Daimler/Knight sleeve valve, water-cooled straight six 105hp at 1,000rpm

Transmission: two-speed and reverse primary box with secondary two-speed selectors on the output shafts

Fuel capacity: 227.3 litres (50 gallons)

Max. speed: 5.9km/h (3.66mph)

Max. range: 37.9km (23 miles)

Fuel consumption: 5.9 litres/km (2.08 gallons/mile)

Trench-crossing capability: 3.5m (11.5ft)

Armament: two 6-pdr (57mm) 40 calibre, QF guns and four 7.62mm Hotchkiss air-cooled machine guns

Muzzle velocity: 554m/sec (1,817ft/sec)

Max. effective range: 6,858m (7,500yds)

Ammunition: solid shot and high explosive

Ammunition stowage: 332 6-pdr; 6,272 7.62mm

MARK I (FEMALE) TANK A11, His Majesty's Landship *We're All in It*, of A Company, Heavy Section, Machine Gun Corps, Somme area, France, November 1916

TANK DETAILS

Previous page: The prototype for the Mark I tank, most commonly known as *Mother*, was developed in Lincolnshire and trialled at Hatfield Park in Hertfordshire, UK. When demonstrated before Lord Kitchener in January 1916 he called it a 'pretty mechanical toy'. *Mother* was unfortunately broken up for scrap following the end of World War I.

This page: A Female Mark I tank in a three-colour camouflage scheme of green, brown and ochre as used during the second half of 1916. The early combat experiences of the tank units of the Heavy Machine Gun Corps were plagued by mechanical difficulties as the tanks broke down or became stranded in trenches and shell holes. By the turn of the year the original batch of tanks was nearly exhausted.

THE MARK IV

The Mark IV could probably be described as the first Main Battle Tank (MBT). Some 1,200 were built and they participated in virtually every British battle on the Western Front from the early summer of 1917 until the very end of the war. The Mark IV was the first tank to be mass produced, the first used en masse in combat, the first built based upon experience with earlier models and the first to be used in a battle planned around the tank.

Production of the Mark IV got underway in March 1917 and now Field Marshal Haig, Commander-in-Chief of the British Expeditionary Force, had high hopes for large numbers of the Mark IV to be available in spring 1917, but production delays prevented this. It would be used in large numbers at the battle of Cambrai (20 November 1917 to 7 December 1917). All nine battalions of the Tank Corps in France took part – a total of 378 fighting tanks. This first large-scale deployment of tanks continues to be celebrated by the Royal Tank Regiment today.

Crews had found the original 'long' 6-pdr of the Mark I too long to be effective in use. There was also a shortage of supply so the Mark IV was equipped with a shortened version – the Ordance Quick Firing (QF) 23-calibre 6-pdr. The gun was a single tube capable of firing much quicker, with a maximum range of 6,675m (7,300yds). Firing solid shot, it was estimated that the gun could penetrate 30mm of armour at 457m (500yds). Lewis light machine guns also replaced the Vickers as the secondary weapon in male tanks and became the main armament on female tanks.

Mechanical improvements were made to the Mark IV tank until the end of the war, including a response to the desire for increased power through better engines. However, by the war's end the tank was already considered obsolete and were mostly used simply as supply tanks with the new Mark V acting as the fighting tank.

SPECIFICATIONS

Crew: 8

Weight: 25.3 tonnes (27.9 tons)

Power-to-weight ratio: 3.7bph/ton

Overall length: 8m (26.2ft)

Overall width (male): 4.11m (13.5ft)

Overall height: 2.43m (8ft)

Engine: Daimler/Knight sleeve valve, water-cooled straight six 105hp at 1,000rpm

Transmission: two-speed and reverse primary box with secondary two-speed selectors on the output shafts

Fuel capacity: 318 litres (70 gallons)

Max. speed: 5.95km/h (3.69mph)

Max. range: 56km (35 miles)

Ground pressure: 12.6km/74.8cm²

Trench-crossing capability: 3.5m (11.5ft)

Fuel consumption: 5.9 litres/km (2.08 gallons/mile)

Armament: two 6-pdr (57mm) 23-cal, QF guns

MARK IV (FEMALE) TANK D51 *DEBORAH* (2ND LT F. G. HEAP), 12th Company, 12th Section, D Battalion, Tank Corps, Cambrai

and four 7.62mm Lewis air-cooled machine guns

Muzzle velocity: 411m/sec (1,348ft/sec)

Max. effective range: 7,300m (7,978yds)

Ammunition: solid shot, high explosive and case

Ammunition stowage (male): 332 6-pdr, 6,272 7.62mm

TANK DETAILS

Previous page: On the first day of Cambrai each of the tanks had a 1.5-ton fascine perched on top of its cab, the only occasion when this device was used by tanks in this way. A fascine is a modest bundle of sticks, but the ones used here were 75 normal fascines bundled together and then squeezed tight by loops of chain. The idea was that each tank would tip the fascine into the extra-wide German Hindenburg Line trenches, enabling it to cross. It was obviously a one-shot commodity.

This page: Some Mark IV tanks included the improved 125hp engine. The improved performance was welcome but it could cause damaged gears hence the use as supply vehicles. They were capable of carrying 5 tons of stores, sufficient to resupply five fighting tanks that might otherwise have been forced to pull out of the battle.

MARK IV SUPPLY TANK
***AULD REEKIE**, Tank Corps
Central Workshops,
France, 1917

THE A7V

The arrival of British tanks on the Western Front in the autumn of 1916 caused some concern within the German Army. Although they had not completely ignored the development of armoured warfare, and had investigated the potential of armoured cars and even started some limited experiments with tracked vehicles, it was clear that the German efforts were some way behind the Allies'. In order to rectify this, a new programme was set up, the Abteilung A7V, named after the 7th Transport Department (Abteilung 7 Verkehrswesen) of the Prussian War Office. This development programme stalled under the weight of demands from other sectors of the German armaments industry until the battle of Cambrai proved the importance of the tank on the battlefield and led to an increased investment and interest in the armour programme.

The design settled on as the most suitable was also known as the A7V, which was armed with a main 57mm gun and six 7.92mm machine guns. It had a large crew of 18, though as many as 24 could be carried. Out of an initial order of 100 tanks only 22 were actually completed as gun tanks, with some of the rest being used to create variants such as anti-aircraft platforms and trench-digging machines.

Trials of the machine were not favourable, as it lacked cross-country performance and mobility. However, it was still committed to combat on 21 March 1918 as part of the great German offensive, Operation *Michael*. Although the appearance of the German armour demoralized the British defenders, the tanks were plagued by mechanical problems. On 24 April 1918, an A7V came under fire from British Mark IV tanks around the town of Villers-Bretonneux in the first tank-versus-tank combat in history. The encounter ended in stalemate with the A7V knocking out two Mark IVs before it had to be abandoned itself. The latter half of 1918 saw the Germans on the defensive and, despite one or two successful minor counter-attacks, the A7Vs fell into state of disrepair and most were captured by the advancing Allies.

A7V-PANZER 506 *MEPHISTO*,
Abteilung 3, Gruppe Uihlein,
Villers-Bretonneux, April 1918

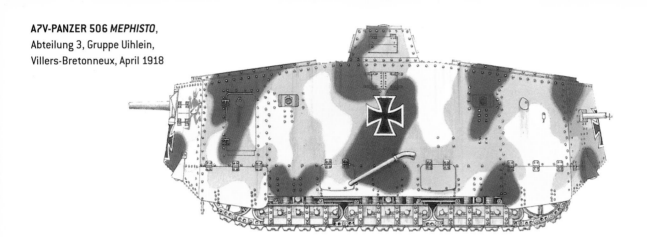

SPECIFICATIONS

Crew: 18+

Weight: 29.9 tonnes (33 tons)

Overall length: 7.35m (24.1ft)

Overall width: 3.06m (10ft)

Overall height: 3.35m (11ft)

Ground clearance: 20cm (7.9in)

Engine/transmission: two Daimler 165-204
100hp 4-cylinder engines, each with sliding
gears

Max. speed: 16km/h (9.4mph)

Max. range (cross-country): 35km (21.74 miles)

Max. range (road): 70km (43.49 miles)

Max. effective range: 6.4km (3.9 miles), initial
muzzle velocity of 487m/sec (1,597ft/sec)

Trench-crossing capability: 2m (6ft 5in)

Armament: 57mm Maxim-Nordenfeldt Model
1888 QF gun, L/26.3 calibre, six 7.92mm
Maschinengewehr 08

Armour: 30mm bow; 15mm sides; 6mm roof

Rate of fire: 20–25 rounds per minute

Ammunition: 100 rounds (50 HE, 30 AP,
20 grape shot); 40–50 ammunition boxes MG
(10,000–15,000 rounds)

TANK DETAILS

Previous page: The A7V *Mephisto* was abandoned by its crew when it became stranded in a shell hole during the battle of Villers-Bretonneux on 24 April 1918. Although efforts were made to demolish the tank it remained in no man's land until the Australians recovered it on 14 July. It was later shipped back to Australia and is the only surviving example of the A7V still in existence.

This page: *Alter Fritz* is shown here in a striking splinter camouflage pattern. This particular tank was knocked out during a counter-attack near Cambrai on 11 October 1918, one of the last hurrahs of the A7V. Its commander, Leutnant Ernst Volkheim, later went on to become the premier historian of the German World War I tank force.

A7V-PANZER 560
ALTER FRITZ,
Abteilung 1,
May 1918

THE MARK V

The Mark V tank entered British service in the closing stages of World War I, first seeing action at the battle of Hamel in July 1918, before playing a vital role in the battle of Amiens and the Hundred Days offensive that led to the armistice in November 1918.

Although intended as an entirely new design, the Mark V ended up being an organic development of the British tank designs that had been refined through Marks I to IV. Externally, at least, there were few differences between the Mark V and its predecessor, the Mark IV. Internally, however, the Mark V was equipped with a totally new engine, designed by the engineer Harry Ricardo, which delivered 150hp rather than the 105hp available for the Mark IV. It also had a new epicyclic transmission that meant that it could now be driven by one man, as opposed to the four required on the Marks I–IV. The Mark V retained the same style of armament as the Mark IV, with the male versions equipped with cut-down 6-pdr QF guns and the female versions mounting only machine guns, though these were now Hotchkiss machine guns rather than Lewis guns.

Following their introduction to the battlefield in the summer of 1918, the new tanks made their name at the battle of Amiens, where virtually the whole Tank Corps was committed in support of a major offensive that took place between 8 and 11 August. Over 340 Mark V and V* tanks took part in the battle, and they proved a vital element in shattering the German forces in what was described by the German general Erich Ludendorff as the 'black day of the German Army'.

The Mark V in its various guises served with the British Army through to the end of the war, as well as equipping some American and French units. The Mark V also saw extensive service with the Allied intervention force in North Russia, and many of them ended up in Soviet hands following the end of the Russian Civil War.

SPECIFICATIONS

Crew: 8

Weight: 26.3 tonnes (29 tons)

Power-to-weight ratio: 5.17bhp/ton

Overall length: 8.05m (26.4ft)

Overall width (male): 4.11m (13.5ft)

Overall height: 2.64m (8.7ft)

Engine: Ricardo crosshead valve, water-cooled straight six 150hp at 1250rpm

Transmission: Wrigley four-speed primary box with independent reverse and Wilson two-speed epicyclics

Fuel capacity: 423 litres (93 gallons)

Max. speed: 7.4km/h (4.6mph)

Max. range: 72km (45 miles)

Fuel consumption: 5.8 litres/km (2.06 gallons/mile)

Ground pressure: 28.7lbs/in^2

Trench-crossing capability: 3.04m (10ft)

Ammunition: solid shot, high explosive and case

A MARK V MALE TANK,
9th Battalion, Tank Corps,
France, 1918

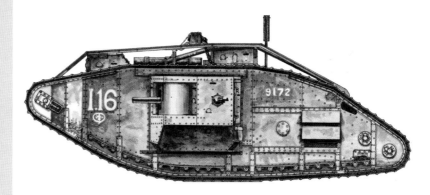

Muzzle velocity (6-pdr): 411m/sec (1,348ft/sec)

Max. effective range (6-pdr): 7,300m (7,978yds)

Armament: two 6-pdr (57mm) 23 calibre, QF guns and four 7.62mm Hotchkiss air-cooled machine guns

Ammunition (male): 207 6-pdr; 5,700 7.62mm

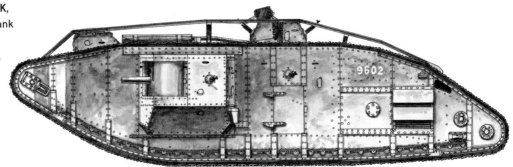

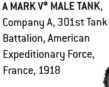

A MARK V* MALE TANK,
Company A, 301st Tank
Battalion, American
Expeditionary Force,
France, 1918

TANK DETAILS

Previous page: The Mark V tank was very similar in design to the Mark IV, but one of the ways to tell the difference is the presence of a distinctive rear cab on the Mark V, as shown here. This particular tank is shown in the markings of the 9th Battalion of the Tank Corps during the battle of Moreuil on 23 July 1918, which was the second time that Mark V tanks were used in action. They were used to support the French 3rd Division and the entire battalion was awarded the *Croix de Guerre* following the action.

This page: The Mark V* was a lengthened variant of the Mark V, designed to cope with the wider trenches of the German Hindenburg Line. This example belongs to the 301st Tank Battalion, part of the American Expeditionary Force and the only American heavy tank battalion to see service during World War I.

THE PANZER III

The Panzer III was the first German medium tank, and as such equipped the Panzer divisions of the Wehrmacht from the early days of blitzkrieg in 1939 and 1940, through the invasion of the Soviet Union in 1941 and the great tank battles of 1943, from which point it began to be removed from front-line service in favour of the Panzer IV and Panther.

Its development started in the 1935 because of a request for a tank large enough to mount a 50mm gun. However, the availability of a 37mm gun already in production meant that this was the weapon adopted, with the tank designed to accommodate an upgrade in weaponry as and when it became available. The early variants (A–E) all mounted the 37mm gun, while later versions (F–M) were generally equipped with a short or long version of the 50mm gun. The final variant, the Ausführung N, mounted a 75mm L/24 howitzer and was used in a fire-support role with Panzergrenadier divisions. The armour protection was initially only 30mm as standard, but this was also gradually increased over the development history of the tank.

Although only 98 early variants of the Panzer III were available for the campaign in Poland in 1939, by the time of the invasion of France in May 1940 nearly 350 had been produced, and it was on the Panzer III that the burden of dealing with the French armour fell, as the German light tanks were not up to the job. The Panzer III succeeded admirably throughout the campaign, and this was probably its finest hour. 1941 saw the tank committed on a number of fronts, with Panzer IIIs forming the main thrust of the German advance into the Soviet Union, while at the same time operating in Greece, the Balkans and North Africa. However, the encounters with KV and T-34 tanks exposed the limitations of the design and the Panzer III declined in significance in favour of heavier German tanks.

PANZER III AUSF. G, DAK, Libya, 1941

SPECIFICATIONS

Crew: 5

Weight: 24.8 tonnes (27.37 tons)

Overall length: 5.41m (17.8ft)

Width: 2.92m (9.6ft)

Height: 2.51m (8.2ft)

Max. speed: 40km/h (25mph)

Max. range: 175km (108 miles)

Engine: Maybach HL 120 TRM V-12 water-cooled
petrol engine, 300hp

Armament: one 50mm KwK L/42 gun with
99 rounds and two 7.92mm machine guns
with 3,750 rounds

Armour: 30mm (hull front); 25mm (glacis);
30mm (driver's plate); 30mm (sides); 17mm
(decking); 16mm (belly); 21mm (tail); 30mm
(turret front, sides and rear); 10mm (top)

Trench-crossing capability: 2.3m (7.5ft)

Vertical step: 60cm (23.5in)

Fording capability: 80cm (31.5in)

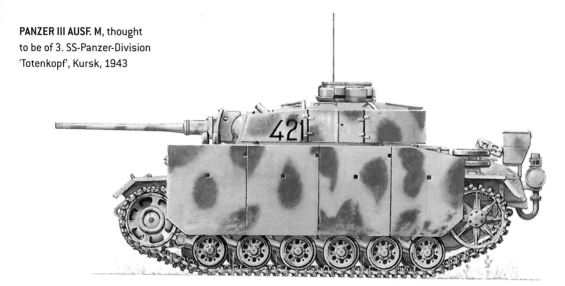

PANZER III AUSF. M, thought to be of 3. SS-Panzer-Division 'Totenkopf', Kursk, 1943

TANK DETAILS

Previous page: Different variants of the Panzer III provided the bulk of the German armour committed to the campaign in North Africa, though their air filters proved unsuitable to the climate and caused many breakdowns. The tank shown is an Ausf. G with the 50mm gun and has been uparmoured with spare tracks and roadwheels.

This page: The Ausf. M was the last 50mm gun-armed variant of the Panzer III, though by this stage of the war it was clear that it was too weakly armed and armoured to play much more of a role in combat. The great tank battles of 1943 were the last time it would form a major part of the order of battle of the Panzer divisions.

THE MATILDA INFANTRY TANK

The Matilda was the dominant tank in the early days of the war in North Africa. Its heavy armour made it practically invulnerable to Italian anti-tank fire, and it wasn't until the Germans arrived in numbers in the theatre that the Matilda became outclassed and eventually obsolete.

Developed in the pre-war years as a tank specifically designed for supporting infantry, the A11 Matilda was to be heavily armoured, speed was not seen as essential. The A11 was only equipped with a machine gun. With the onset of war it was decided to increase the tank's firepower, and the A12 was equipped with a 2-pdr anti-tank gun and a co-axial machine gun, though only solid shot was provided and no high-explosive. This tank, the Matilda Mark I, was upgraded following the Fall of France, with the Besa machine gun replacing the Vickers on the Mark II and the Mark III featuring an improved engine and transmission system.

The Matilda equipped two Army tank battalions during the battle for France in 1940, with 77 A11 and 23 A12 tanks in 4th and 7th Battalions Royal Tank Regiment. The British tanks were unsuited to the war of movement imposed upon them by the German blitzkrieg tactics and, although they were largely invulnerable to the German 37mm anti-tank gun, they were often knocked out by German artillery fire. They also suffered heavily from mechanical and track failures. Every single tank committed to the campaign was abandoned in France when the BEF (British Expeditionary Force) was evacuated.

It was in the North African desert that the Matilda found its true role, being christened the 'Queen of the Desert'. In the battles of late 1940 and early 1941 against the Italians the A12 Matilda outclassed the Italian armour and was immune to their anti-tank fire, providing a key component in the British advance across Libya. With the arrival of German forces the Matilda's days of dominance were over, but the tank continued to play a vital role through to June 1942 and even took part in the first battle of El Alamein in July.

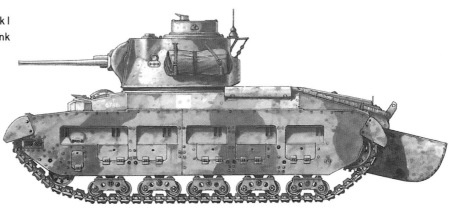

INFANTRY TANK A12, Matilda Mark I
Gamecock, 7th RTR, 1st Army Tank
Brigade, BEF, France, 1940

SPECIFICATIONS

Crew: 4

Combat weight: 26.9 tonnes (29.7 tons)

Power-to-weight ratio: 7.2 hp/ton

Overall length: 6.02m (19.8ft)

Width: 2.59m (8.5ft)

Height: 2.52m (8.3ft) (high cupola)

Max. speed: 24km/h (15mph)

Max. range: 80km (50 miles) on internal tank

Engine: two Leyland Type E148 and E149 straight
6-cylinder water-cooled diesels, each 95bhp at
2,000rpm

Transmission: Wilson six-speed pre-selector
gearbox and Rackham steering clutches

Fuel capacity: 181.8 litres (40 gallons), plus
163.6 litres (36 gallons) in auxiliary tank

Fuel consumption: 2.2 litres/km (0.78
gallons/mile)

Fording capability: 1m (3.2ft)

Armament: ordnance QF 2-pdr (40mm) Mark IX
(52-cal), co-axial Besa 7.92mm air-cooled
machine gun

Ammunition: AP solid (1kg)

Muzzle velocity: 853m/sec (2,798ft/sec)

Max. effective range: 1,828.8m (6,000ft)

Ammunition stowage: 93 rounds

Gun depression/elevation: -20 / +20 degrees

INFANTRY TANK MARK II,
Matilda Mark III *Gulliver II*,
7th RTR, Libya, 1941

LIVER II T.6923

TANK DETAILS

Previous page: This Mark I Matilda of 7th RTR is shown in the camouflage scheme used by the BEF in France 1940. The Matilda was ill suited to the type of war waged during the French campaign, though it did cause the Germans some consternation during the British counter-attack at Arras on 21 May before being halted by German 88mm guns.

This page: Another Matilda of 7th RTR, this time a Mark III in the Western Desert. The unusual colour scheme was designed to break up the outline of the tank and confuse enemy gunners, an idea inspired by World War I experience. The Western Desert proved much more suitable for the Matilda's attributes, and the tank dominated the battlefield in the early days of the campaign.

THE M3 LEE/GRANT MEDIUM TANK*

The M3 medium tank was rushed into production in 1941 as a stopgap measure to satisfy the desperate need for a medium tank in US and British tank forces. Its design was a messy stew of outdated inter-war design features and time-saving shortcuts. To its credit, it was one of the best-armed tanks of its day and it was based on sound automotive design. The M3 was a godsend to British armoured divisions in the spring and summer of 1942 because of its good armour and heavy firepower, something that current British tank designs sorely lacked. Its powerful 75mm gun could penetrate contemporary Panzer armour, and it was also capable of dealing with the deadly 88mm anti-tank guns.

The M3 entered combat at the turning point of the war against Germany in North Africa. It was used by the British Eighth Army in the 1942 battles at Gazala, Alam Halfa and El Alamein, and later took part with both British and US tank units in the final defeat of the Afrika Korps in Tunisia in 1943.

By the time production reached full stride in early 1942, the more mature M4A1 Sherman tank was entering production, which quickly replaced the M3 on the assembly lines.

The M3 was ultimately an interim solution until more effective tank designs could be produced. Despite its strange design and severe tactical disadvantages, it proved effective on the battlefield due to its dual-purpose armament and powerful main gun. Called 'the tank that surprised Rommel', it gave a boost to faltering Allied morale just as it seemed that German armour was insurmountably superior to anything the Allies could field.

While the M3 disappeared from the tank role in the European theatre by mid-1943, it continued to serve in more distant theatres such as Burma. Its chassis formed the basis for a number of specialized armoured vehicles, such as the widely used M31 tank-recovery vehicle. The last Lee/Grant tanks remained in service until the mid 1950s in such diverse locations as Brazil and Australia.

* The American version was called the 'Lee', after General Robert E. Lee, and the British version was called the 'Grant', after General Ulysses S. Grant.

GRANT CRUISER TANK,
22nd Armoured Brigade,
Gazala, May 1943

Max. range: 193km (120 miles)

Fuel consumption: 3.9 litres/km
(1.4 gallons/mile)

Ground clearance: 43cm (17in)

Armament: 75mm M2 gun in M1 mount in hull;
37mm M6 gun in M24 combination mount in
turret with co-axial .30-cal machine gun; two
.30-cal Browning machine guns in hull

Muzzle velocity: 75mm gun: 1,930ft/sec (APC);
37mm gun: 2,900ft/sec (M51 APC)

Penetration: 75mm M61 APC = 60mm at 500yds
at 30 degrees; 37mm M51 APC = 53mm at
500yds at 30 degrees

Max. effective range: 75mm: 13,600yds; 37mm:
12,850yds

Gun depression/elevation: 75mm: -9 / +20
degrees; 37mm: -7 / +60 degrees

Armour: 51mm (turret mantlet and turret sides);
51mm (hull front); 38mm (hull sides)

SPECIFICATIONS

Combat weight: 27.8 tonnes (30.7 tons)

Power-to-weight ratio: 11.3hp/ton

Overall length: 5.6m (18.4ft)

Width: 2.7m (8.9ft)

Height: 3.10m (10.2ft)

Engine: Continental R975 EC2 radial 340hp
9-cylinder gasoline engine with 973in³
displacement

Transmission: synchromesh transmissions
with five forward and one reverse gears

Fuel capacity: 795 litres (175 gallons)

Max. speed (road): 38.6km/h (24mph)

Max. speed (cross-country): 24km/h (15mph)

TANK DETAILS

Previous page: The M3's most distinctive feature is its tall silhouette. The hull-mounted 75mm gun had a limited traverse compared to the much less effective 37mm turret above it, but it did give British armour the firepower it needed to counter Rommel's superb Panzer forces. This tank is the British-modified Grant version of the M3.

This page:
In 1945, Lees operating in Burma had several modifications, notably appliqué armour in the form of spare track links on the hull front and various welded plates on the hull side and the

sides of the engine compartment to protect against lunge-mines. The markings here are fairly typical, including a white Allied star, a vehicle name and the usual tactical insignia at the 5 and 8 o'clock positions of the turret rear.

LEE CRUISER TANK,
C Squadron, 150th Regiment
RAC, Burma, 1945

THE PANZER IV

The Panzer IV has a reputation as the 'work horse' of the German Panzer forces in World War II. While it did not have the sleek appearance of the Panther, nor the awe-inspiring bulk of the Tiger, it could get the job done. Developed from October 1935, the Panzer IV with the short-barrelled 7.5cm KwK L/24 was highly successful in its intended combat role as an infantry-support tank, living up to its code name of 'Begleitwagen' (escort tank – abbreviated to B.W.) by providing effective high-explosive fire. After encountering the Russian T-34/76 and KV-1 tanks in the summer of 1941, however, the troops wanted a tank that could knock out enemy tanks at long range. This version of the Panzer IV was created by replacing the short-barrelled gun in the turret with a long-barrelled 7.5cm KwK 40 L/43 or L/48.

The Panzer IV has the distinction of being the only German tank to remain in continuous production throughout World War II. Even in 1945 it was still a highly effective battlefield weapon and the match of any British or US counterpart. It was not until July 1944 that Shermans equipped with the 76mm gun began to appear, finally matching the Panzer IV in firepower. The Panzer IV made up roughly half of all German tanks in use on the Western Front in 1944–45, and played a major part in the Ardennes Offensive, where their good mobility and ability to cross difficult terrain enabled them to spearhead the push into the enemy lines. After the failure of this operation the tank was only encountered again in declining numbers, most of the crumbling German defence relying on small battlegroups built around a few assault guns or Panzerjäger.

Though by 1945 it was eventually outclassed by its brothers the Panther and Tiger, and outgunned by the Russian IS series and the new T-34/85, the Panzer IV remained in use right up until the end of the war. It even saw action in 1965, employed by the Syrian Army against Israeli Centurions.

SS-DIVISION 'LSSAH', France, 1942

SPECIFICATIONS

Combat weight: 25 tonnes (27.6 tons)

Power-to-weight ratio: 10.6 metric hp/tonne

Overall length: 7.02m (23ft)

Width: 2.88m (9.4ft)

Height: 2.68m (8.8ft)

Max. sustained speed (road): 25km/h (15.5mph)

Average speed (cross-country): 20km/h (12.4mph)

Max. speed: 38–42km/h (23–26mph)

Max. range (road): 320km (199 miles)

Max. range (cross-country): 210km (130 miles)

Trench-crossing capability: 2.3m (7.5ft)

Fording capability: 0.8m (2.6ft)

Step climbing: 0.6m (1.9ft)

Ground clearance: 0.4m (1.3ft)

Ground pressure: 0.89kg/cm^2

Steering ratio: 1.43

Engine: 11.9-litre V-12 Maybach HL 120 TRM 265 metric hp at 2,600rpm

Fuel capacity: 680 litres (150 gallons)

Track on ground: 3.52m (11.5ft)

Transmission: S.S.G.76, six forward, one reverse gears

Armament: 7.5cm KwK 40 L/48; 7.5cm Pzgr. 39 (armour-piercing); 7.5cm Pzgr. 40 (armour-piercing – tungsten core); 7.5cm Pzgr. Sprgr. (high explosive)

Sight: T.Z.F.5f

Stowed main-gun rounds: 87

Stowed main-MG rounds: 3.150

TANK DETAILS

Previous page: From mid-1940 to early 1943 all German Army vehicles were painted in a single colour – Dunkelgrau, RAL 7021 (dark grey) – with the exception of vehicles sent to hot climates from the spring of 1941. The Balkankreuz (black cross with white outline) was painted on either side of the superstructure and on the rear of the armour guard for the smoke grenade rack on the rear of the motor compartment.

This page: This Panzer IV has the 7.5cm KwK 40 L/48 gun, which proved effective against almost all Allied tanks. This tank has mesh aprons (Drahtgeflechtschürzen) attached to its sides to break up hollow charge rounds before they hit the main armour. The same principle is behind the spaced armour around the turret, which is designed to reduce the velocity of armour piercing rounds and make them lose their penetrative power.

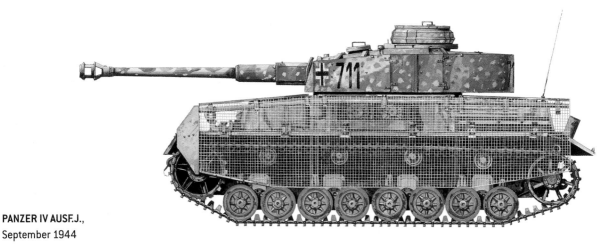

PANZER IV AUSF.J.,
September 1944

THE CRUSADER CRUISER TANK

The Crusader tank came into British service in 1941, seeing combat action in the North African desert. Ultimately, it was born out of a flawed design concept inherited from the pre-war British Army that separated tank designs into 'infantry' and 'cruiser' types, but it fulfilled a role until other, better designs could be introduced.

The Crusader's official designation was the 'Tank, Cruiser, Mark VI' and it was developed from an earlier cruiser tank the A13 by Nuffield Mechanization and Aero in Birmingham, which provided the basic design for both the Covenanter (the Mark V) and the Crusader. The tank was sent straight to production, and was ready for issue by May 1941, being sent to the Western Desert immediately.

The Crusader mounted a 2-pdr main gun, with a co-axial Besa machine gun. The Mark VI also had another Besa in an auxiliary turret to the front left of the tank. The armour plate was initially only 30mm thick, though this was increased on later variants, while the tank was powered by a Nuffield Liberty Mark III V-12 engine that was plagued with mechanical issues in operational use.

Issued to 6th Royal Tank Regiment in May 1941 the Crusader was sent straight into action in North Africa, taking part in Operation *Battleaxe* in June, the failed attempt to relieve Tobruk. The more successful Operation *Crusader* of June 1941 featured an entire armoured brigade, the 22nd, equipped with the tank. Combat use revealed that the Crusader was both underarmoured and undergunned in comparison to its German adversaries, though its speed was impressive. It also suffered from major reliability problems. Although attempts were made to increase the armour protection and lethality of the tank, including fitting a 6-pdr gun to the turret, by the end of the campaign in North Africa the Crusader had been declared obsolete and all British regiments equipped with it were re-equipped with Shermans. The chassis continued to be used for other purposes, including anti-aircraft and self-propelled guns.

CRUSADER MARK I, 3rd RTR,
8th Armoured Brigade,
10th Armoured Division

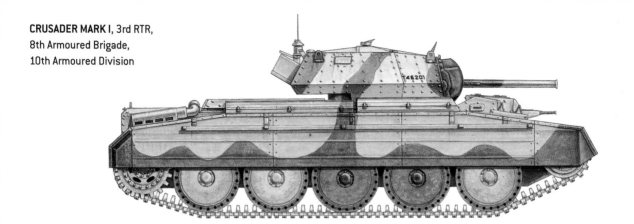

SPECIFICATIONS

Crew: 3

Combat weight: 19.8 tonnes (21.8 tons)

Power-to-weight ratio: 20.2 bhp/ton

Overall length: 5.98m (19.6ft)

Width: 3.52m (11.5ft)

Height: 2.24m (7.3ft)

Engine: Nuffield Liberty Mark III/IV V12,
water-cooled, 340bhp at 1,500rpm

Transmission: Nuffield constant mesh four-speed
gearbox and Wilson dual regenerative epicyclic
steering, air operated

Fuel capacity: 500 litres (200 gallons),
plus 136 litres (30 gallons) in auxiliary tank

Max. speed: 43km/h (26.7mph)

Max. range: 177km (110 miles) on main tank

Fording capability: 0.96m (3.1ft)

Fuel consumption: 2.8 litres/km (0.99
gallons/mile)

Armament: 6-pdr, 7cwt QF Mark III (57mm);
co-axial 7.92mm Besa air-cooled machine gun

Ammunition: AP, APC, APCBC, HE

Muzzle velocity: 853m/sec (2,799 ft/sec)

Max. effective range: 1.83km (6,000ft)

Ammunition stowage: 65 rounds

Gun depression/elevation: -12.5 / +20 degrees

**CRUSADER MARK II COMMAND
TANK TAURUS, HQ 11th**
Armoured Division

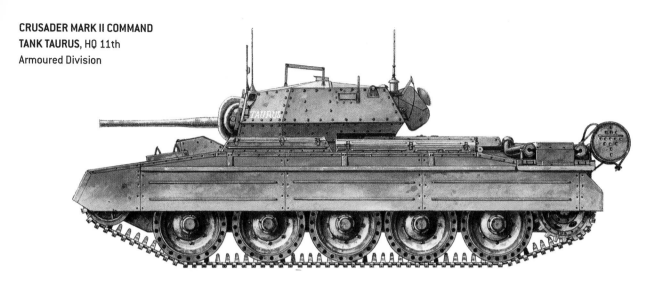

TANK DETAILS

Previous page: This Crusader Mark I is equipped with the auxiliary machine-gun turret that proved difficult to use and was removed on later variants. 3rd RTR fought with the Crusader during the Alamein battles of 1942 before taking part in the Tunisian campaign.

This page: This plate shows a command tank of the 11th Armoured Division in Britain. Command tanks can be identified through the proliferation of aerials needed for the quantity of radio equipment carried. The main gun was removed and replaced by a convincing dummy.

THE T-34/76

The T-34 was the most influential tank design of World War II. When first introduced into combat in the summer of 1941, it represented a revolutionary leap forward in tank design. Its firepower, armour protection and mobility were superior to that of any other medium tank of the period and it was the most widely produced Allied tank of the war. The inspiration for the T-34 came from lessons learnt during the Spanish Civil War, where the Soviet government had dispatched several shipments of tanks to Spain. Foremost was the need for more armour protection, as little had changed since World War I, and Soviet tanks were easily penetrated by German 37mm anti-tank guns. This lesson was reinforced in 1938 and 1939 during clashes with the Japanese Army.

German troops began encountering T-34 tanks from the first day of the Operation *Barbarossa* campaign. They came as a great shock to the German infantry, whose 37mm anti-tank gun projectiles simply bounced off the T-34's armour at ranges of over 300m. In their dispatches, German field commanders began to mention the 'tank terror' that struck the infantry when Red Army tanks appeared. Despite their great impact on morale, the T-34 crews were too inexperienced to use the new tank effectively. One crew, after being fired upon 23 times by a German anti-tank gun to little effect other than to jam the turret ring, didn't even manage to hit their opponent. Many T-34 crews, either through poor training or lack of ammunition, preferred crushing these guns under their tracks.

The heyday of the T-34 came in the summer of 1943, during the battles in the Kursk–Orel salient. By this time the tank had lost much of its technical superiority, but Soviet tactics were now much more sophisticated and crews were more skilled. Moreover, the Red Army had adopted a doctrine of using overwhelming numbers to defeat the better-quality German tanks. Although in one-on-one encounters the T-34 usually came away worse off than its most common counterpart, the Panzer IV, the sheer number of T-34s on the battlefield meant that these tank formations were highly effective.

T-34 MODEL 1941, Separate Tank Brigade, autumn 1941

SPECIFICATIONS

Crew: 3

Combat weight: 25.4 tonnes (28 tons)

Power-to-weight ratio: 17.5–19hp/ton

Hull length: 6.1m (20ft)

Overall length: 6.73m (22.1ft)

Width: 2.92m (9.6ft)

Engine: V-2-34 diesel, 4-stroke, 12-cylinder, 500hp at 180rpm

Transmission: dry multi-plate main clutch, mechanical gearbox, one-stage side drives with side clutches and strap brakes, four forward, one reverse gears

Fuel capacity: 673 litres (148 gallons) internal plus two external 45-litre (10-gallon) fuel cells

Max. speed (road): 54.7km/h (34mph)

Max. speed (cross-country): 26–40km/h (16–25mph)

Cruising speed: 29km/h (18mph)

Max range: 467km (290 miles)

Fuel consumption: 1.8 litres/km (0.65 gallons/mile)

Fording capability: 1.27m (4.2ft)

Armament: F-34 76.2mm tank gun (42 calibres long)

Muzzle velocity: 655m/sec (2,150ft/sec) (BR-350A APHE)

Max. effective range: 2.4km (1.5 miles)

Stowed main gun rounds: 77 rounds

Gun depression/elevation: -3 / +30 degrees

Secondary armament: Degtaryev DT 7.62mm machine gun, co-axial DT 7.62mm machine gun

Armour: 47mm (hull front); 45mm (hull sides); 45mm (hull rear); 65mm (turret front); 65mm (turret sides); 47mm (turret rear)

TANK DETAILS

Previous page: During World War II, Soviet tanks were uniformly painted very dark green. Markings usually appeared in white. By August 1941, efforts were being made to increase morale. One aspect of this effort was the decision to encourage units to paint patriotic slogans on the sides of tanks. In this case, the Russian word is 'Pobeda', or 'Victory'.

This page: Soviet workers were encouraged to contribute part of their salaries towards the purchase of weapons. Often, once a certain sum was collected, a ceremony would be held to commemorate the donations. In this case, the 112th Tank Brigade was re-equipped with T-34 Model 1943 tanks in January 1943 bought by Mongolia.

T-34 MODEL 1943, 112th Tank Brigade, 6th Tank Corps, January 1943

THE M4 SHERMAN

Named by the British after a celebrated Union Army general of the American Civil War, Sherman was the generic name for all tanks in the American M4 medium series. Second only to the Soviet T-34 (see pp.36–38) in terms of quantity and longevity of service, it was far more varied than its Russian contemporary amounting virtually to five different tanks.

These were: the M4 (British Sherman I), the M4A1 (British Sherman II), the M4A2 (British Sherman III), the M4A3 (British Sherman IV) and the M4A4 (British Sherman V).

These tanks were distinguished primarily by the type of engine fitted. The M4 and M4A1 used the Continental nine cylinder air-cooled radial as in the M3 Lee/Grant (see pp.27–29) although the M4A1 was easily recognized by its rounded, cast hull. THe M4A2 used twin General Motors six cylinder diesel engines, the M4A3 a reliable gasoline Ford V8 and the M4A4 the troublesome Chrysler multi-bank, a 30 cylinder petrol engine built up from five six cylinder truck engines all bolted together.

All types except the M4A1 having the slab-sided, welded hull. However, in late production Shermans new hull forms were adopted along with a revised suspension named "easy-eight."

In terms of armament, once again, there were many variations; the original weapon was the dual purpose 75mm gun M3 which was perfectly adequate for the proposed role of the tank although it was later supplemented by a 105mm howitzer for close-support work. To enhance the Sherman's anti-tank capability a high velocity 76mm weapon in an enlarged turret was introduced in 1944 while the British managed to squeeze their 76.3mm (17-pdr) gun into the original Sherman turret to create the Firefly (see pp.40–50)

In addition to its service with the Americans and the British, the Sherman was also supplied in large numbers to the Canadians, South Africans, French and Soviet armies both during and after World War II. The Sherman even fought in the Korean War and with the new Israeli Defence Force where it was adapted, modified and improved in many ways.

SPECIFICATIONS

Crew: 5

Combat weight: 31.5 tonnes (34.8 tons)

Power-to-weight ratio: 12.2hp/ton

Hull length: 6m (19.7ft)

Overall length: 6m (19.7ft)

Width: 2.6m (8.5ft)

Engine: 4,25hp Chrysler A57 multibank engine

Transmission: synchromesh, five forward,
    one reverse gears

Fuel capacity: 727 litres (160 gallons)

Max. speed (road): 40km/h (25mph)

Max. speed (cross-country): 32km (20mph)

Max. range: 161km (100 miles)

Max. effective range: 1.28km (0.8 miles)

Fuel consumption: 4.5 litres/km
    (1.6 gallons/mile) (cruising)

Fording capability: 106cm (42in)
    (without preparation)

M4A1, G CO., 1st Armd. Regt.,
US 1st Armd. Div., Sidi-bou-Zid,
Tunisia, February 1943

Main-gun ammunition: M61 APC
    (armour-piercing), M89 white
    phosphorous, M48 high explosive

Armament: 75mm M3 gun in M34 mount

Stowed main gun rounds: 97

M61 APC muzzle velocity: 618m/sec
    (2,030ft/sec)

Gun depression/elevation: -12 / +8 degrees

TANK DETAILS

Previous page: This Sherman has the distinctive rounded hull and turret of early models. Note the single hatch for the tank commander. If the crew had to bail out the loader had to crawl under the gun breech and use the commander's hatch. Later models incorporated an additional hatch for the loader. The small port on the turret side was used to dispose of spent shell casings.

This page: A good example of a heavily sandbagged tank. These modifications were frequently carried out by engineer companies, which finished the job off by repainting the whole vehicle, sandbags and all. Here the Sherman is painted in the most common scheme – No. 10 Black sprayed over No. 9 Olive Drab.

THE PANTHER MEDIUM TANK

The origins of the Panther tank lay in the shock that the German Army experienced during Operation *Barbarossa* – its June 1941 invasion of the Soviet Union. The Soviets' T-34/76 medium tank outclassed every German tank then in service. Beginning in November 1941, the 'Panther Commission' commissioned several prototypes to counter this threat, culminating in the 15 May 1942 decision to contract the production of the Panzerkampfwagen V Panther, the first mass-produced Panther tank. Entering service in January 1943, Germany now had an excellent medium tank, and one that would become one of the most feared vehicles of the war.

Perhaps the most impressive aspect of the Panther was its lethality, even at long range. Firing the PzGr.39/42 and 40/42 armour-piercing rounds at a normal combat range of 1,000m, the Panther could penetrate 111mm- and 149mm-thick armour at an angle of 30 degrees, which was enough to deal with nearly all enemy tanks. The other great strength of the Panther was its battlefield survivability, which rested mainly on its thick, well-sloped frontal armour. The Soviet T-34/85 could only penetrate this at a range of 500m, and the 75mm-gunned Sherman M3A2 could not do so even at point-blank range. This created a situation in which the Panther could confidently destroy almost any enemy tank at long range whilst its opponent needed to either close to dangerously short ranges or manoeuvre around to the Panther's sides or rear, where the Panther had much weaker armour.

The Panther was rushed into combat during the 1943 battle of Kursk before it was fully ready, and therefore it suffered from a number of teething problems in its early battlefield use. Throughout the final years of the war, however, the Panther was an excellent medium tank that saw use on both fronts, and its effectiveness prompted the Allies to design heavier tanks to counter it, such as the M-26 Pershing and Soviet IS-2. Its use late in the war undoubtedly enabled the German Army to resist overwhelming Allied pressure for significantly longer than would otherwise have been possible.

LATE MODEL D PANTHER OF 13. PANZER-DIVISION IN THREE-TONE CAMOUFLAGE, Eastern Front, autumn 1943

SPECIFICATIONS

Crew: 5

Weight: 45.5 tonnes (50 tons)

Overall length: 8.86m (29.1ft)

Overall width (male): 3.3m (10.8ft)

Overall height: 2.95m (9.7ft)

Engine: Maybach HL 230 P30 V-12 liquid-cooled petrol, 690hp

Max. speed: 55km/h (34mph)

Max. range: 177km (110 miles)

Trench-crossing capability: 1.9m (6.2ft)

Vertical step: 90cm (35.4in)

Fording capability: 1.4m (4.6ft)

Armament: 75mm KwK 42 (L/70) gun with 79 rounds and two 7.92mm MG 34 machine guns with 4,500 rounds

Armour: 80mm (hull front); 50mm (sides); 40mm (rear); 15mm (decking); 20 + 13mm (belly); 110–20mm (turrent front); 45mm (sides and rear); 15mm (top)

TANK DETAILS

Previous page: This is a late Model D Panther. It only has one headlamp, on the left, it lacks the circular communications hatch fitted to the left-hand side of the turret and it has improved tracks with chevron cleats for the muddy conditions on the Eastern Front during autumn. The drum-shaped gun mantlet is a distinctive feature of this Panther variant.

This page: Features that identify this tank as a Model G, late-production vehicle are the distinctive 'chin' fitted to the bottom of the mantlet to prevent incoming rounds being deflected down onto the thin hull roof, together with a modified driver's periscope and altered rear hull decking. The tank has been painted in the relatively uncommon 'splinter' design, with large straight-edged blocks of Dark Olive Green and Red-Brown painted over a base of Dark Yellow.

**LATE MODEL G PANTHER
IN LINEAR SPLINTER
CAMOUFLAGE**, Poland,
autumn 1944

THE TIGER I HEAVY TANK

Probably the most famous tank of World War II, the Tiger I was quickly designed utilising components that had been partially tested in previous heavy Panzers. While limited development of heavy Panzer designs had commenced in 1937, the first serious efforts resulted from a meeting with Hitler on 26 May 1941. Design of the Tiger I was thus not initiated as a response to the T-34 and KW tanks encountered during Operation *Barbarossa* in June 1941. Instead, the main concerns addressed during the meeting were the problems of successfully combating British tanks and anti-tank guns. However, after the appearance of the T-34 and KW, the design and production of an effective heavy Panzer was pursued with increased urgency.

Although the Tiger I was an extremely powerful weapon, it brought with it many problems, not least of which was its great weight, which limited the bridges it could cross and thus operational mobility. It was also a highly complex machine and prone to breakdowns. The Tiger was designed as an offensive weapon, but by the time it was used on the battlefield Germany was on the defensive, and the Tiger was rushed from place to place to lend its heavy firepower to the defence, often exacerbating its mechanical problems.

Nevertheless, the Tiger I was extremely successful in combat with other tanks. In the East this is reflected in reports from the 503. and 506. schwere Panzer Abteilung. From the beginning of the battle of Kursk on 5 July until 21 September 1943 the 503. claimed to have destroyed 501 enemy tanks, 388 anti-tank guns, 79 artillery pieces and seven aircraft. On the Western Front, the British and Americans had no tank that could go toe-to-toe with the Tiger, and tank crews dreaded encountering it. The Tiger could only be defeated at extremely close range by Allied tank guns, and the Sherman Firefly variant was designed as a direct counter to German heavy-tank designs. The Tiger's effectiveness was limited by the small numbers available and the overwhelming numerical superiority of Allied armour, but it nevertheless remains one of the most successful tanks of World War II.

TIGER I, 1.Kompanie/schwere Heeres Panzer Abteilung 502, near Leningrad, January 1943

SPECIFICATIONS

Crew: 5

Combat weight: 58 tonnes (64 tons)

Power-to-weight ratio: 12.3 metric hp/ton

Ground pressure: 0.735kg/cm²

Overall length: 8.45m (27.7ft)

Width: 3.7m (12.1ft)

Engine: Maybach HL 230 P45 V-12 petrol

Transmission: Maybach Olvar Type OG 40 12 16 B, eight forward, four reverse gears

Max. speed (road): 45.5km/h (28.3mph)

Max. speed (cross-country): 15–20km/h (9–12mph)

Best cruising speed: 38km/h (23.6mph)

Max. range: 195km (121 miles) at cruising speed

Sight: Turmzielfernrohr 9c (Monocular, magnification 2.5x and 5x)

Fording capability: 1.6m (5.2ft)

Armament: 8.8cm KwK 36 L/56

Main-gun ammunition: 8.8cm PzGr 39 (armour-piercing), 8.8cm PzGr 40 (armour-piercing, tungsten core), 8.8cm Gr 39 (hollow charge)

Muzzle velocity: 773m/sec (2,536ft/sec) (PzGr 39)

Stowed main gun rounds: 92

Gun depression/elevation: -9 / +10 degrees

TANK DETAILS

Previous page: This Tiger, tactical number 100, belonging to the company commander, was the first Tiger captured intact by the Russians in January 1943. A large reproduction of the 502nd emblem, a *Mammut* (mammoth), had been painted on the rear of the turret. The stowage bin on the turret side was made and fitted by the troops at the front.

This page: The schwere Heeres Panzer Abteilung 505 had one of the most spectacular non-regulation markings. They painted their unit emblem, a knight on a charger, on both turret sides. The exact colours used for this emblem cannot be confirmed but from photographs several different colours were used that may have been changed to identify company or platoon affiliation. The tactical number, normally painted on the turret side, was stencilled onto the main gun's armoured sleeve and on the rear of the turret bin. It is also fitted with very resilient steel-rimmed road wheels.

TIGER I, schwere Heeres Panzer Abteilung 505, Russia, February 1944

THE SHERMAN FIREFLY

During 1942 the British Eighth Army in North Africa began to receive large numbers of American M4 Sherman tanks. However, the Allies were well aware that the Sherman could not match up to the powerful German tanks that were beginning to enter production, such as the Panther. With its high-velocity L-70 calibre 75mm armament the Panther was capable of destroying a Sherman tank at twice the previous combat range in any one-on-one encounter. As such, three or four Shermans were often lost in order to destroy just one Panther or Tiger. By 1943, the British had developed the highly effective 17-pdr anti-tank gun, which had a performance comparable to the 75mm gun of the Panther. At the time, there was no British tank design capable of mounting such a heavy weapon due to the limited size of their turrets. As an interim measure, hundreds of Shermans were fitted with the 17-pdr by mounting the weapon on its side and extending the turret at the rear. This model was known as the Sherman Firefly and eventually represented almost one in every four tanks in British units. The Firefly was still very similar externally to the standard Sherman, with the glaring exception of the much longer barrel of the 17-pdr, which overhung the front of the vehicle; this made the Firefly stand out among standard Shermans. The Germans soon learnt to knock out any Fireflies they encountered before tackling the standard Shermans, an unwelcome surprise for many British tank crews who received the new tank at short notice and with little training.

Nonetheless, the Firefly still had formidable killing power particularly when armed with APDS (Armour Piercing Discarding Sabot) ammunition, which had the potential to penetrate even the thick, sloped frontal armour of the massive Tiger II at ranges of up to 1,500yds. In one of the most impressive tank duels of the war a Sherman Firefly managed to dispatch three Tigers with just five rounds thanks to the accurate fire of Trooper Joe Ekins of the 1st Northamptonshire Yeomanry.

SPECIFICATIONS

Crew: 4

Combat weight: 31.5 tonnes (34.75 tons)

Overall length: 7.8m (25.6ft)

Width: 2.6m (8.5ft)

Height: 2.7m (8.9ft)

Engine: Chrysler A57 multi-bank

Transmission: five-speed synchomesh and
controlled differential steering

Fuel capacity: 727 litres (160 gallons)

Armament: 17-pdr Mark IV QF gun and .30cal
Browning machine gun

Ammunition stowage: 77 rounds

Muzzle velocity: 883m/sec (2,900ft/sec)

Max. effective range: 2.3km (1.4 miles)

Gun depression/elevation: -5 / +20 degrees

Speed: 36km/h (22.25mph)

Max. armour thickness: 7.62cm (3in)

TANK DETAILS

Previous page: An entirely standard Firefly with some interesting details. Brackets holding jerry cans have been fitted to each side of the turret radio box and patches of appliqué armour have been welded to the side of the hull. They added 1in to the tank's armour.

This page: A Polish Firefly with patches of appliqué armour covering the regular areas but not the turret and with the gun barrel camouflage paint effect. It is shown crossing a Churchill ARK – a redundant Churchill tank hull that was used to provide a causeway for other tanks to cross in difficult terrain. The Firefly also carries a fascine for use in a muddy ditch.

SHERMAN IC HYBRID FIREFLY *ZEMSTA II* (*REVENGE*) OF C SQUADRON,
1st Krechowiecki Lancers, 2nd Polish
Armoured Brigade, Italy, 1944

THE T-34/85

The T-34/85 tank is one of those rare weapons that have remained in service for more than half a century. First introduced in 1944, it has seen combat in nearly every corner of the globe. Although long obsolete in Europe, it has proven a reliable and potent weapon in many Third World conflicts.

The Red Army began to receive the T-34/85 tank in March 1944. In general, preference was given to Guards formations. The aim was to completely re-equip each brigade with T-34/85s, but in fact many brigades remained mixed formations with both the older T-34 and the newer tank. T-34/85s made their combat debut in late March 1944 during operations in western Ukraine. The tank's arrival was a relief to Soviet tankers, for although the T-34/85 did not reverse the German technical advantage in tank armour and firepower, it nearly matched it. A major advantage the Soviet tank did have was in strength of numbers. At the end of May 1944 the Wehrmacht had only 304 Panthers on the Eastern Front, whilst production of the T-34/85 was running at about 1,200 per month. The success of the new design was proved by their use in Operation *Bagration*, in which they contributed decisively to the defeat of Army Group Centre.

Nowhere was the combat employment of the T-34/85 more pivotal than in the Korean conflict in 1950. When the North Korean People's Army invaded the South in June 1950, their T-34/85s gave them an unparalleled offensive capability in a region where armoured vehicles were rare. South Korean infantry had no effective weapon to counter this tank, which led to demoralization and 'tank panic', fatally weakening the Republic of Korea's defences.

Korea was to prove the last conflict in which the T-34/85 had a major impact. By the early 1950s, the T-54A was available in quantity, and the T-34/85 became increasingly obsolete. But in the 1950s and 60s the T-34/85 was widely used in successive Middle Eastern conflicts, including the 1956 Suez Canal Crisis and the 1967 Six Day War.

T-34/85 MODEL 1943,
38th Separate Tank Regiment,
53rd Army, Umansko-Botoshankskiy
Operation, 29 March 1944

SPECIFICATIONS

Crew: 5

Combat weight: 31.7 tonnes (35 tons)

Power-to-weight ratio: 14.2hp/ton

Hull length: 6.1m (20ft)

Overall length: 8.1m (26.6ft)

Width: 3m (9.9ft)

Engine: V-2-34 diesel, 4-stroke, 12-cylinder 500hp
at 1,800rpm

Fuel capacity: 545 litres (120 gallons) internal,
270 litres (59 gallons) external

Transmission: dry multiplate clutch, mechanical
gearbox, one stage side drives with side
clutches and strap brakes, four forward,
one reverse gears

Max. speed (road): 55km/h (34mph)

Max. speed (cross-country): 30km/h (18.5mph)

Max. range (road): 300km (186 miles)

Fuel consumption: 2.7 litres/km
(0.95 gallons/mile)

Fording capability: 1.3m (4.3ft)

Armament: 85mm ZiS-S-53 gun (54.6 cal long)

Main-gun ammunition: BR-365 armour-piercing;
BR-365P sub-cal armour-piercing; OF-365 high
explosive/fragmentation

Muzzle velocity: 1,200m/sec (BR-365P)

Max. effective range: 13.3km (8.3 miles)

Stowed main gun rounds: 55–60

Gun depression/elevation: -5 / +25 degrees

Secondary armament: hull-mounted and co-axial
DTM 7.62mm machine guns

Armour: 90mm (turret front); 75mm (turret
side); 75mm (turret rear); 47mm (hull glacis);
60mm (hull side); 47mm (hull rear)

T-34/85 MODEL 1953 (CZECHOSLOVAK PRODUCTION), 44th Armoured Brigade, Syrian Army, Ein Fite, Golan Heights, 10 June 1967

TANK DETAILS

Previous page: This was one of the first T-34/85 units to see combat, and it was initially deployed in the winter of 1944 around the key road junction at Balta (Ukraine), near the Romanian border. The tanks were named *Mitriy Donskoi* after the legendary Muscovite tsar (1359–89), who vanquished the Tartars at Kulikovo in 1380. Funds to purchase the tanks were collected by the Russian Orthodox Church.

This page: The Syrian Army made a large purchase of T-34/85s from Czechoslovakia in the mid-1950s. These tanks have the characteristic Czechoslovak turret casting shape, the guard over the front headlights and the infantry signal fairing on the rear of the left hull side. Syrian vehicles were left in dark olive green, essentially the same colour used by Warsaw Pact forces at the time.

THE CHURCHILL INFANTRY TANK

The Churchill is one of the most well known examples of the British 'infantry tank' concept. The basic requirement of this design was armour heavy enough to withstand the fire of any anti-tank gun known to be in service during the design phase, and firepower consistent with its task; speed was not considered to be an essential quality, since the pace of any engagement would be geared to that of the infantry. The Churchill was envisioned to fight on a battlefield similar to that of the Western Front in 1918, and was given a wide trench-crossing capacity and the ability to drive over the worst shell-torn ground. The design incorporated a high top run for the tracks, so the vehicle's hull contained a hint of its World War I ancestors.

On the virtues and vices of the Churchill its crews were unanimous. They welcomed the stout armour and the sponson escape hatches, the tank's ability to climb the steepest hills and wallow through the deepest mud, and the additional stowage space permitted by the wide hull, but they regretted the absence of a main armament that would put them on equal terms with German tank crews.

The Churchill came into its own in the close country of the Normandy bocage, with its banked hedgerows and patchwork of small fields, where they played a vital role in supporting the infantry. The tank's multiple-bogey suspension came into its own here, and enabled it to cross terrain that no other tank could. Churchills played a particularly decisive role in the capture of Hill 309 on 30 July 1944. In the course of a single day the Churchills of the 6th Guards Tank Brigade covered 10km (6 miles) across country over close bocage, a feat which many felt could only have been performed by Churchills.

The Churchill was also used successfully in North Africa, Italy, Western Europe and even in Korea in the 1950s. In later years it had been up-gunned to mount a 6-pdr main gun, and the late model Churchill Mk VII had considerably more armour than even the German Tiger I.

SPECIFICATIONS

Crew: 5

Combat weight: 35.3 tonnes (39 tons)

Power-to-weight ratio: 8.75 hp/ton

Hull length: 7.44m (24.4ft)

Overall length: 7.44m (24.4ft)

Height: 2.44m (8ft)

Width: 3.25m (10.7ft)

Engine: Bedford Twin-Six 350hp

Transmission: Merrit-Brown four-speed gearbox

Steering: Controlled differential

Max. speed (road): 25km/h (15.5mph)

Max. speed (cross-country): 13km/h (8mph)

Fording capability: 1m (3.3ft) (without preparation)

Vertical obstacle: 76cm (2.5ft)

Armament: 6-pdr gun (Ordnance QF Mk III)

Main-gun ammunition: 6-pdr APC (Armour-Piercing with Cap), 6-pdr APC BC

CHURCHILL MARK III OF 'KINGFORCE', El Alamein, October 1942

(Armour-Piercing with Cap, Ballistic Cap), 6-pdr APDS (Armour-Piercing Discarding Sabot)

Muzzle velocity: 903m/sec (2,965ft/sec)

Armour penetration: 81mm at 460m with target at 30 degrees

Stowed main gun rounds: 84

Gun depression/elevation: -12.5 / +20 degrees

Previous page: This view clearly shows the distinctive large tracks of the Churchill tank. The overall finish of sand yellow is camouflaged with disruptive patches of dark blue-grey – probably the colour 'Slate Grey No. 34'. 'Kingforce' was given the tactical number '510' scrawled in black on a piece of cardboard and fastened to the front of the nearside track. The canvas apron was used to prevent the 'Sirocco' fan drawing in dust through the tank's hatches.

This page: One of the major limitations of the Churchill's design was its small turret, which prevented large guns being fitted to it. This relative lack of firepower was to remain a problem throughout World War II. This tank has had local mud daubed on it in a tigerstripe pattern in order to break up its outline.

CHURCHILL MARK III,
145 Regt. RAC,
Tunisia, 1943

THE KV-1 HEAVY TANK

The KV was born out of a desire following World War I for a heavy tank to assist in break-through operations. During the 1930s Russia experimented with several tank designs but they were generally too heavy or impractical for use in combat. A May 1938 meeting led to a redesign of previous models, and the new tank was given the name 'KV', after Marshal Klimenti Voroshilov, the People's Defence Commissar. On 19 December 1939 the Defence Committee accepted the KV for service as the Red Army's new heavy tank. An initial production batch of 50 tanks was ordered for delivery in 1940 with a redesigned turret.

The German Wehrmacht launched Operation *Barbarossa* on 22 June 1941. The next day, Panzer units faced KV tanks for the first time. The KV's heavy armour proved impervious to anything the Germans could fire at them. Not only were the 37mm tank guns of the PzKpfw 35(t)s ineffective, but more frightening was the fact that 75mm fire from 'Stubs' (PzKpfw IVs with short 75mm guns) also proved ineffective, the most powerful weapon used on German tanks of the period. Some KVs simply crushed the enemy anti-tank guns by running them over, using the heavy weight of their vehicle as a weapon to make up for having no ammunition. Major General K. Rokossovskiy recalled in his memoirs: 'The KV tanks literally stunned the enemy. They withstood the fire of every type of gun the German tanks were armed with. But what a sight they were on returning from combat. Their armour was pock-marked all over and sometimes even their barrels were pierced.'

In spite of the exceptional performance of the KV tanks on many individual occasions, their overall impact on the 1941 fighting was negligible. Their technical superiority could not overcome the overwhelming tactical and operational shortcomings of the Red Army. The most obvious problem was the lack of training for the crews, which compounded the frequent mechanical failures. At the time of their introduction, the average service life for new Soviet tanks was 1,000–1,500km (620–930 miles) before factory rebuilding was necessary.

KV-1 MODEL 1941 (UP-ARMOURED TURRET) 12TH TANK REGIMENT,
1st Moscow Motor Rifle Division, August 1942

SPECIFICATIONS

Crew: 5

Combat weight: 42.6 tonnes (47 tons)

Power-to-weight ratio: 13hp/ton

Hull length: 6.8m (22.3ft)

Overall length: 7m (23ft)

Width: 3.3m (10ft 11in)

Engine: V-2K 4-stroke, V-type, 500hp at 180rpm, 38.8-litre diesel engine

Fuel capacity: 600 litres (158 gallons) internal

Transmission: dry multi-plate main clutch, sliding-mesh gearbox, multi-plate clutch braking turning mechanism, five forward, one reverse gears

Max. speed (road): 34km/h (21mph)

Max. speed (cross-country): 16km/h (10mph)

Max. range: 249km (155 miles)

Fuel consumption: 2.4 litres/km (1 gallon/mile)

Fording capability: 1.6m (5.2ft)

Armament: 76.2, ZIS-5 rifled tank gun, 42 cal long; three 7.62mm DT machine guns

Main-gun ammunition: BR-350A armour-piercing; OF-350 HE/frag; Sh-350A shrapnel

Muzzle velocity: 655m/sec (2,150ft/sec) (BR-350A)

Max. effective range: 2.4km (1.5 miles)

Stowed main gun rounds: 135 rounds

Gun depression/elevation: -4 / +24 degrees

Armour: 75mm (hull basis); 75mm + 26mm (hull nose); 75mm + 31mm (glacis); 40mm (belly); 32mm (hull rear); 95–100mm cast (turret front and sides); 30mm (turret roof)

TANK DETAILS

Previous page: This particular tank was commanded by Lieutenant Pavel Khoroshilov and was renamed *Bezposhadniy* ('Merciless'). It was paid for by contributions from Moscow artists who had won the Stalin Prize. During the presentation ceremony, it was colourfully marked and sported a large cartoon of a Soviet tank firing on Hitler.

This page: In the autumn of 1942, the 5th Guards Heavy Tank Regiment was given 21 new KV-1S tanks. They were marked with the inscription *Sovyetskikh Polyarnik* ('Soviet Arctic Explorers'). This particular tank was rebuilt in May 1944, and served with the 3rd Ukrainian Front during the Yassi-Kishniev battles in southern Ukraine.

THE CHURCHILL CROCODILE FLAMETHROWER TANK

The British had experimented with flamethrower weapons during Word War I, and they saw extensive use in 1940 during the preparations for a potential German invasion under the aegis of the Petroleum Warfare Department. It was perhaps inevitable that these weapons should be mounted on vehicles, and then tanks. In 1941 Ronson flame projectors were mounted on universal carriers, while in 1942 two of these flame projectors were mounted on the new Churchill tank, which became known as the Churchill Oke after one of the officers involved in the conversion. Three of these Churchills accompanied the Canadian forces on the ill-fated Dieppe raid of August 1942. The flamethrower concept was revised, with a trailer being used to carry the flame fuel so that the normal fighting capabilities of the tank were not impaired. This resulted in the development of the Churchill Crocodile.

Based on the Churchill Mark VII, this mounted the Wasp II flame projector, which replaced the hull machine gun. The system was powered by high-pressure nitrogen carried in an armoured fuel trailer, which could be jettisoned if hit.

The new flamethrower tank equipped three regiments of the 31st Armoured Brigade, part of the 79th Armoured Division that contained so much of the specialized armour used in the campaign in Northwest Europe. The first Crocodiles went ashore on D-Day with 141st Regiment RAC, and later supported US units during their assault on the fortifications at Brest. Crocodiles were also used in Italy with the 25th Armoured Engineer Brigade, where in conjunction with Canadian Wasp flamethrower carriers they supported the crossing of the river Senio on 9 April 1945 so successfully that the attacking 2nd New Zealand Division suffered no casualties at all. The Crocodile remained in use after the end of World War II, and C Squadron, 7th RTR, was sent to Pusan in 1950 as part of the British contribution to the UN effort. However, they never operated in the role of flamethrowers in Korea, only as normal gun tanks.

CHURCHILL MARK II OKE FLAMETHROWER *BEETLE*

OF 8 TROOP, B Squadron, 14th Canadian Army
Tank Regiment, Dieppe, 19 August 1942

SPECIFICATIONS

Crew: 5

Combat weight: 41.7 tonnes (46 tons)

Overall length: 12.3m (40.4ft)

Height: 2.4m (7.9ft)

Width: 3.2m (10.5ft)

Engine: Bedford Twin-Six 350bhp

Transmission: Merrit-Brown H41

Fuel capacity: 682 litres (150 gallons)

Max. speed: 21km/h (13mph)

Max. range: 144km (89 miles)

Fording capability: 1m (3.2ft) (without preparation)

Armament: 75mm Mark V and 7.92mm Besa machine gun

Ammunition: 84 rounds

Muzzle velocity: 618m/sec (2,028ft/sec)

Effective range: 1.8km (1.1 miles)

Gun depression/elevation: -12.5 / +20 degrees

Flame fuel capacity: 1,818 litres (400 gallons)

Flame fuel consumption: 21 litres/sec (4.6 gallons/sec)

Effective range: 100.5m (330ft)

TANK DETAILS

Previous page: An early variant of the Churchill flamethrower tank, the Oke mounting the Ronson flame projector, was used to support the Canadian landing at Dieppe in August 1942. Three of the tanks – *Bull*, *Boar* and *Beetle* – were launched, but *Bull* was swamped, *Boar* managed to knock off its armoured fuel tank and so could not use its flamethrower, and *Beetle* successfully got ashore but then broke a track.

This page: A Churchill Crocodile tank as used in the fighting for Holland in January 1945. A coat of whitewash has been applied over the top of the camouflage pattern on both the tank and the trailer, though it has already started to wash off this particular tank.

CHURCHILL VII CROCODILE,
A Squadron, 7th Royal Tank
Regiment, Holland,
January 1945

THE KING TIGER HEAVY TANK

The Tiger II tank, produced from February 1944, was the ultimate heavy tank of World War II. The imposing name of *Konigstiger* has been variously translated as King Tiger or Royal Tiger which summed up the awe with which the tank was held by Allied troops. But the tank was more prosaically known as the Tiger II. It was one of the heaviest, most thickly armoured and powerfully armed tanks of the war. Like the Tiger I, the Tiger II paid for its power with increased weight and mechanical problems. By the time it was entering a battlefield role on the Western Front it was generally used in a static defensive role, mitigating this disadvantage somewhat, but it did prove problematic during the Ardennes Offensive.

The Tiger II's 8.8cm KwK 43 (L/71) was a very accurate gun capable of first-round hits at ranges exceeding 1,000m. It was also extremely powerful, and capable of penetrating 193mm of armour at a range of 1,000m. Along with its extremely effective main gun, the Tiger II's major asset was the thick front armour. Even the side and rear armour protection was sufficient to eliminate any serious threat from the American 75mm or Russian 76mm tank guns.

The Tiger II was first used in combat in July 1944 in Normandy and subsequently on the Eastern Front. As was the case with the Tiger I and Panther, US and British tanks had a difficult time engaging it from the front, as they lacked any heavy tanks of their own. Only the up-gunned British Sherman Firefly firing APDS ammunition could penetrate its frontal hull and turret armour. The main problem the Tiger IIs had was a lack of sufficient numbers to make a significant impact on the war, and a lack of well-trained crew, as by this stage the Wehrmacht was reaching the limit of its manpower reserves. Crews who had never used a Tiger II were assigned to them when they were already on their way to the front. This exacerbated mechanical problems as crews were unfamiliar with their vehicles.

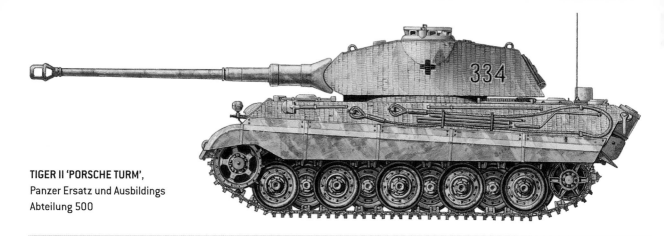

TIGER II 'PORSCHE TURM',
Panzer Ersatz und Ausbildings
Abteilung 500

SPECIFICATIONS

Crew: 5

Combat weight: 69.7 tonnes (76.9 tons)

Power-to-weight ratio: 10.7 metric hp/ton

Hull length: 6.4m (21ft)

Overall length: 10.29m (33.8ft)

Width: 3.76m (12.3ft)

Engine: Maybach HL 230 P30 V-12 petrol, 700hp

Fuel capacity: 860 litres (189 gallons)

Max. speed (road): 38km/h (23.6mph)

Max. speed (cross-country): 15–20km/h
(9–12.5mph)

Max. range: 170km (105mph) (cruising speed)

Max. effective range: 10km (6.2 miles)
(SprGr 40/43)

Fuel consumption: 5 litres/km
(1.77 gallons/mile)

Armament: 8.8cm KwK 43 L/71

Transmission: Maybach Olvar Type OG 40 12 16 B,
eight forward, four reverse gears

Main-gun ammunition: 8.8cm PzGr 39/40
(armour-piercing, tungsten core), 8.8cm
PzGr 40/43 (armour-piercing, tungsten core),
8.8cm SprGr 43 (high explosive), 8.8cm
HlGr 39 (hollow charge)

Muzzle velocity: 1,000m/sec (3,280ft/sec)

Gun depression/elevation: -8 / +15 degrees

TANK DETAILS

Previous page: The Panzer Ersatz und Ausbildungs 500 (Replacement and Training Battalion 500) was equipped with some of the earliest production Tiger IIs. At this period all Tiger IIs were coated in Zimmerit anti-mine paste, as it was thought that magnetic anti-tank mines could be a threat. The commander's cupola, dwarfed by the turret, gives an idea of the sheer size of the tank.

This page: This tank crew has removed a rectangle of Zimmerit from the turret side and therein painted their unit emblem, a knight on a charger. The Tiger II combined the thick armour of the Tiger I with the sloped frontal armour of the Panther, giving it unprecedented battlefield survivability. A towing cable can be seen attached to the side of this tank.

TIGER II, schwere Panzer Abteilung
505, Thüringen, 1944

THE CROMWELL CRUISER TANK

The Cromwell tank replaced the Crusader as the principal cruiser tank in the British armoury, and proved to be a much more successful design. It saw extensive service in the last years of World War II, mainly with the cavalry reconnaissance regiments.

As early as the battle for France it was clear that British tanks were undergunned and armoured in comparison to their German adversaries, but the necessity of keeping an armoured force in being following the BEF's evacuation from France ensured the continuation of obsolete tank programmes. Although interim designs dominated the ranks of British armour in the mid-war years, by 1943 better tanks such as the Cromwell were coming into mass production. Initially mounting the 6-pdr gun, which was later rebored to take American 75mm ammunition in order that a high-explosive shell could be used, the Cromwell was powered by the excellent Rolls-Royce Meteor engine that gave it an impressive top speed of over 60km/h (37mph).

The Cromwell saw service for the first time in Normandy, where it equipped the entire 7th Armoured Division as well as the cavalry reconnaissance regiments. A rival variant – known as the Centaur – was also used on D-Day itself as a close-support weapon for the Royal Marines. A lengthened Cromwell chassis mounting the 17-pdr gun, known as the Challenger, was also developed to provide heavy anti-tank support. The reliability and speed of the Cromwell was impressive, with the 7th Armoured Division advancing some 110km (68 miles) in one day following the Normandy breakout. However, the gun was still underpowered when compared to the German Tiger and Panther tanks and efforts were made to upgrade the design with a shortened version of the 17-pdr gun, resulting in the Comet tank, which came into service in November 1944. The Cromwell and Comet continued to be used in the post-war period, with many Cromwells being upgraded with a 20-pdr gun and renamed the Charioteer.

CROMWELL MARK VW, 5th Royal Tank Regiment, 22nd Armoured Brigade, 7th Armoured Division, Normandy, 1944

SPECIFICATIONS

Crew: 5

Combat weight: 27.4 tonnes (30.3 tons)

Overall length: 6.4m (21ft)

Width: 3.05m (10ft)

Height: 2.48m (8.1ft)

Engine: Rolls-Royce Meteor V-12 liquid-cooled petrol, 600hp

Max. speed: 61km/h (38mph)

Max. range: 278km (173 miles)

Fording capability: 1.22m (4ft)

Armament: 75mm Mark V or VA gun; two 7.92mm Besa air-cooled machine guns

Ammunition: 64 rounds main gun; 4.950 rounds machine gun

TANK DETAILS

Previous page: This Cromwell is part of the 7th Armoured Division, the only whole formation to be completely equipped with Cromwells during the campaign in Northwest Europe. As befits a veteran unit, the tank is loaded down with extra stores and equipment, as well as the foliage-style camouflage adopted during the hedgerow fighting in Normandy.

CROMWELL MARK IV, King's Own Hussars,
7th Armoured Division, Operation *Blackcock*,
January 1945

This page: Operation *Blackcock* involved some bitter fighting in harsh winter conditions along the Dutch/German border. Tanks were given a rough coating of whitewash to reduce contrast with the snowy landscape, and this obliterated all the usual markings. Although the 8th Hussars were nominally the reconnaissance regiment, by this stage of the war they had become the de facto fourth armoured regiment of the 22nd Armoured Brigade.

THE M48 PATTON

The M48 Patton tank design arose out of the M26 Pershing, which served in the last months of World War II. With the intensification of the Cold War in the late 1940s the US Army began a general modernization of its armoured forces. A rebuilt derivative of the M26 was accepted for Army service in 1948 as the M46 Patton tank. The new design was essentially similar to the M26 except for a new CD-850 cross-drive transmission and an AV-1790-5A engine. Although not realized at the time, this engine and transmission package would form the heart of American tank designs for nearly 35 years until the advent of the M1 Abrams in 1981.

In April 1952 the first production-model M48 Patton rolled off the assembly lines at Newark, Delaware. The M48 and the slightly improved M48A1's greatest tactical deficiency was its short operational range of only 112km (70 miles). While actually slightly better than its contemporaries, such as the Centurion, this made necessary the use of a jettisonable rack on the rear hull, which could carry four 250-litre (55-gallon) fuel drums. Many of the M48 and M48A1 tanks were exported through Military Assistance Program, and M48A2 became the standard US Army and US Marine tank of the late 1950s and 1960s.

The M48 was the main battle tank of the US Army and Marine Corps during the Vietnam War, where it saw extensive combat in the more low-lying east of the country and in urban operations. It performed well in an infantry-support role, but there was little enemy armour for it to engage. The M48 offered good protection from enemy small-arms fire and even RPGs, and it was found that it could survive landmine impacts with only minor damage. The M67 variant was equipped with a powerful flamethrower that was useful in the confined terrain of Vietnam. It was nicknamed the 'Zippo' after the brand of cigarette lighter. The M48 has been used extensively in the Middle East as well, notably in the 1967 Six Day War and the Indo-Pakistani Wars.

SPECIFICATIONS

Crew: 4

Combat weight: 48.5 tonnes (53.5 tons)

Power-to-weight ratio: 14.1hp/ton

Overall length: 8.7m (28.5ft)

Width: 3.6m (11.9ft)

Height: 3.3m (10.8ft)

Engine: Continental AVDS-1790-2A 750hp

Transmission: cross-drive CD-850-6A with single-stage multiphase hydraulic torque converter

Fuel capacity: 1,750 litres (385 gallons)

Max. speed (road): 48km/h (30mph)

Max. speed (cross-country): 40km/h (25mph)

Max. range: 482km (300 miles)

Fuel consumption: 3.67 litres/km (1.3 gallons/mile) (cruising)

Ground clearance: 42cm (16.5in)

Armament: 90mm gun M41 in M87A1 mount

Main-gun ammunition: 62 rounds 90mm gun

PAKISTANI M48, 6th Armoured Division, Sialkot Sector, 1965

Muzzle velocity: M332A1 APDS 914m/sec (3,000ft/sec)

Max. range: 21km (13 miles)

Gun depression/elevation: -9 / +19 degrees

Penetration: M332A1 APDS = 160mm; M348 HEAT = 190mm

Armour: 110mm front upper hull; 76mm front sides; 114mm gun mantlet; 178 turret front; 76mm turret sides

TANK DETAILS

Previous page: This M48 in Pakistani service carries a white band around the turret as a means of distinguishing it from Indian tanks. This practice did not become widespread until the 1971 war, when both sides were using much the same equipment. Note the large rounded turret and the stowage basket running around its rear.

This page: The M48 was the last US tank to mount a 90mm gun, which can be seen here with its distinctive muzzle brake. There is a personal name ('Tula') on the barrel as well as a personal insignia, a white Maltese cross, on the canvas searchlight cover and on the bow. This tank has additional protection around the commander's cupola to protect him from small-arms and shrapnel fire.

USMC, M48A3, 1ST MARINE TANK BATTALION, Operation *Badger Tooth*, Quang Tri, Vietnam, January 1968

THE SHERMAN DD AMPHIBIOUS TANK

Sherman DD (Duplex Drive) tanks, or Swimming Shermans, were a key part of the operational plan for D-Day, as it was thought vital to have armoured support for the infantry on the beaches. These vehicles were designed to 'swim' under their own power from craft off the shore in order to land alongside the first waves of infantry.

The efforts to develop a tank with an amphibious capacity had started in the pre-war years, but it was the work of one man – Nicholas Straussler – that revolutionized the field. Working originally with British tank designs such as the Tetrarch and the Valentine, Straussler decided to retain the original tank largely unmodified and construct a waterproof canvas screen around the upper half of the tank, creating a canvas hull and improving the vehicle's buoyancy. The tank was then driven through the sea by the use of propellers powered by the main engine.

In 1943 the Sherman tank replaced the British types in the DD programme, and by the time of the D-Day landings five British and Canadian armoured regiments and three US tank battalions were equipped with different variants of the Sherman DD.

Their performance on D-Day itself was mixed; the British 13th/18th Hussars off Sword Beach landed 31 out of the 34 tanks they launched, while off Gold Beach the Sherwood Rangers lost eight tanks and the 4th/7th Dragoon Guards never got to test the sailing qualities of their tanks as their LCT ran them all the way in. The Canadians off Juno Beach saw 21 out of 29 make it to the shore, while the US 70th Battalion off Utah Beach only lost one tank on the way in. However, off Omaha Beach it was a different story with only two out of the 29 tanks of the 741st Battalion making it to the shore. Swimming Shermans were used again in the campaign in Northwest Europe both in operations in the Scheldt Estuary and in the crossing of the rivers Rhine and Elbe in Germany.

SHERMAN V DD, A SQUADRON, 13th/18th
Royal Hussars, Normandy, 6 June 1944

SPECIFICATIONS

Crew: 5

Power-to-weight ratio: 10.7hp/ton

Combat weight: 34.4 tonnes (38 tons)

Overall length: 7.31m (24ft)

Overall width: 3.2m (10.5ft)

Overall height (screen raised): 3.8m (12.5ft)

Ground clearance: 20cm (7.9ft)

Engine: General Motors 6046, 12-cylinder twin-in-line diesel 410hp at 2,900rpm

Transmission: five-speed and reverse gears, controlled differential steering

Max. speed (land): 48km/h (30mph)

Max. speed (water): 8km/h (5mph)

Max. range: 241km (150 miles)

Armament: 75mm M3, two M1914 .30-cal Browning machine guns

Muzzle velocity: 618.7m/sec (2,027ft/sec)

Max. effective range: 9.7km (6 miles)

Ammunition: 97 rounds

Gun depression/elevation: -10 / +25 degrees

TANK DETAILS

Previous page: The British landings off Sword Beach were supported by the DD tanks of the 13th/18th Royal Hussars, as shown here. This particular tank has now reached shallow water so has dropped the front of its canvas screen to engage German targets. At the rear of the screen is a blue/green and white checkerboard recognition pattern.

This page: DD tanks were not only used in Northwest Europe. This example comes from the Italian Theatre where they were used for river-crossing operations and in the advance on Venice in May 1945, where this tank of the 7th Queen's Own Hussars is pictured.

SHERMAN III DD, B Squadron, 7th Queen's Own Hussars, Venice, May 1945

THE M24 CHAFFEE LIGHT TANK

The M24 Chaffee entered service with the US Army towards the end of World War II, replacing the outdated M3 and M5 series of light tanks. In the short time it saw combat in the war it proved to be an excellent design and went on to see widespread use throughout the world in the post-war era.

One of the main problems with the M3 and M5 light tanks was that they lacked a suitable main armament, mounting only a 37mm gun. So when the M24 was developed it was equipped with a 75mm weapon, which in turn meant that the armour was kept light in order to keep to a weight limit of 18,144kg (20 tons). The power train was very similar to that used in the M5A1, with only minor alterations. Developed throughout 1943, the tank went into production in April 1944 and the first batch of M24s arrived in France in early December 1944, just in time to take part in the Battle of the Bulge. Only two Chaffees actually took part in the battle, being attached to the 740th Tank Battalion.

The new tank made an immediately favourable impression, with its mobility and main gun being praised, though tankers had reservations about its level of armour protection and it was clear that the tank was not suitable for use against enemy armour. As a result it was used primarily in a reconnaissance role.

By the end of the war just over a third of US light tanks were M24 Chaffees, while a significant number were also used by the British. Since World War II the tank has been used by the US in Korea and exported widely, seeing service with the French in Indochina, perhaps most famously at the battle of Dien Bien Phu, and also with the Pakistani Army in their wars against India in 1965 and 1971. The M24 remains in use with the Uruguayan Army to this day.

M24 LIGHT TANK, Company D, 36th
Tank Battalion, 8th Armored Division,
Rheinberg, Germany, March 1945

SPECIFICATIONS

Crew: 5

Combat weight: 18.3 tonnes (20.2 tons)

Power-to-weight ratio: 14.6hp/ton

Overall length: 5.5m (18ft)

Width: 2.98m (9.8ft)

Height: 2.77m (9.1ft)

Engine: two Cadillac 44T24 8-cylinder, 4 cycle
engines, 148hp each at 3,200rpm

Transmission: Hydramatic with four speeds

Fuel capacity: 500 litres (110 gallons)

Max. speed (road): 56km/h (35mph)

Max. speed (cross-country): 32km/h (20mph)

Max. range: 161km (100 miles)

Fuel consumption: 3.1 litres/km
(1.1 gallons/mile)

Ground clearance: 46cm (18in)

Armament: 75mm M6 gun in M64 mount; .30-cal
machine gun; two .30-cal machine guns

Main-gun ammunition: 48 rounds 75mm;
440 rounds .50-cal; 3,750 rounds .30-cal

Muzzle velocity: 6,197m/sec (2,030ft/sec)
(M61APC)

Penetration: 66mm at 500yds at 30 degrees
obliquity

Max. effective range: 12.8km (8 miles)

Gun depression/elevation: -10 / +15 degrees

Armour: 38mm (gun mantlet); 25mm (turret
sides); 25mm (hull upper front); 25mm
(hull lower front); 25mm (hull sides)

TANK DETAILS

Previous page: An M24 Chaffee with typical late-war US markings and painted in lustreless olive drab. This particular vehicle was knocked out during the fighting for the German town of Rheinberg on 3 March 1945, when Company D lost 17 out of its 18 M24s in the battle for the heavily defended town.

This page: The M24 was supplied to Pakistan as a replacement for their M3 and M5 tanks and saw considerable service in their conflicts with India. This particular example has a light-grey camouflage pattern over the olive drab, with a white band around the turret to aid recognition.

M24 LIGHT TANK,
29th Cavalry,
Pakistan Army,
Boyra, Bangladesh,
November 1971

THE M3 AND M5 STUART LIGHT TANK

The M3 and M5 family of tanks, known to the British as the Stuart, were the first US-built tanks to see active service in World War II. Developed in the 1930s, they were nearing obsolescence by the beginning of World War II, but continued to be used in a variety of roles right through to the end of the war in 1945.

During the inter-war years the US Army paid scant attention to the development of armoured vehicles, investing only in a limited number of combat cars and light tanks. However, France's shock defeat in 1940 provoked the US Army into the realization that its armoured forces were under-equipped for modern combat and required new organization and vehicles. Although medium tanks were what was required, the US armaments industry was not set up to provide them and so light tanks would have to fill the gap. The M3 light tank was based on the existing M2A4 light tank, but with improved armour protection and a 37mm gun. This was the first US tank to see service, with the first shipment of tanks, now known as the Stuart, reaching British forces in the Western Desert in July 1941 in time for Operation *Crusader*. Their combat performance was mixed, with the crews praising their mechanical reliability and speed, but criticizing the poor armour protection and inadequate main armament. In late 1941 the M3 also saw service with US forces in the Philippines, and it proved better suited to the conditions in the war in the Pacific.

Throughout 1941 and 1942 the M3 went through a series of upgrades, culminating in the M5 light tank, introduced in autumn 1942. The new model had a redesigned hull and was now powered by twin Cadillac engines. By this stage, it was clear that the M3 and M5 series were unsuitable for tank-versus-tank combat, at least in the European and Mediterranean theatres, and they were increasingly used in a reconnaissance role where they could use their speed to its advantage. In the Pacific they retained their equality with Japanese armour and remained in use throughout the war.

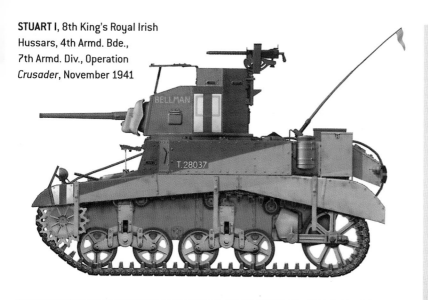

STUART I, 8th King's Royal Irish Hussars, 4th Armd. Bde., 7th Armd. Div., Operation *Crusader*, November 1941

with two optional 114-litre (25-gallon) jettisonable fuel tanks

Max. speed (road): 58km/h (36mph)

Max. speed (cross-country): 32km/h (20mph)

Max. range: 120km (75 miles)

Fuel consumption: 3.7 litres/km (1.3 gallons/mile)

Ground clearance: 42cm (16.5in)

Armament: 37mm M6 gun in M22 combination mount with co-axial .30-cal machine gun and four .30-cal Browning machine guns

Main-gun ammunition: 103 rounds of amour-piercing, M51 APC, M63 high explosive, M2 canister (60 per cent HE, 30 per cent AP, 10 per cent canister)

Muzzle velocity: 884m/sec (2,900ft/sec) (M51APC)

Max. effective range: 11.7km (7.3 miles)

Gun depression/elevation: -10 / +20 degrees

Armour: 51mm (gun mantlet); 38mm (turret sides); 38mm (hull upper front); 44mm (hull lower front); 25mm (hull sides)

SPECIFICATIONS

Crew: 4

Combat weight: 12.4 tonnes (13.7 tons)

Power-to-weight ratio: 18.2hp/ton

Overall length: 4.5m (14.8ft)

Width: 2.2m (7.2ft)

Engine: Continental W-670-90A radial 7-cylinder gasoline engine 667in 3 displacement

Transmission: synchromesh, five forward, one reverse gears

Fuel capacity: 255 litres (56 gallons) internal

TANK DETAILS

Previous page: An early M3 Stuart in British service during Operation *Crusader*, November 1941. This tank is camouflaged in the Caunter scheme designed to break up its outline. Stuarts suffered heavily in the *Crusader* fighting, with the 8th Hussars losing 20 of them in their first day of combat on 19 November 1941.

M5A1, 601st Tank Destroyer Bn.,
Volturno River, Italy,
October 1943

This page: By 1943 it was clearly realized that the M3 and M5 tanks were no match for German amour and they were used instead for reconnaissance and other duties. In this instance this M5A1 is being used by a tank-destroyer battalion instead of the normal M8 armoured car.

THE CENTURION UNIVERSAL TANK

The Centurion was originally developed out of the desire to have a British tank capable from the outset of mounting the 17-pdr gun. The first Centurion prototypes were delivered in April 1945, with the first trials taking place immediately after VE-Day. The first tanks entered production with the 17-pdr gun but were quickly followed by some 20-pdr prototypes. This became the standard variant in use with the British Army, designated the Mark 3. It also made use of a revolutionary form of armour-defeating ammunition – APDS (Armour Piercing Discarding Sabot). The 20-pdr gun loaded with the APDS round had twice the penetration capability of the fabled 88mm AP round of World War II. It was introduced as standard with the Mark 3 in 1948 and this, combined with the Centurion's excellent fire-control system, ensured that the British were confident of its ability to tackle any of the Soviet tanks on the other side of the Iron Curtain.

The Centurion saw its first combat service during the Korean War (1950–53). Despite the extreme winter conditions the tank performed well and the Centurions of the 8th Hussars won lasting fame when their tanks covered the withdrawal of the 29th Brigade in heroic fashion in the face of the overwhelming spring offensive. Following Korea several improvements were made to the tank. The L7 105mm gun was introduced following trials in Germany in 1959. It was also widely purchased by Britain's allies including Canada, Sweden and Israel. Centurions were at the spearhead of the Israeli Armoured Divisions' capture of the Sinai Peninsula during the Six Day War (1967). Infrared night driving and fighting equipment were also introduced and an improved Israeli version of the tank – designated SHO'T – provided valiant service during the Yom Kippur War (1973), although it was eventually phased out in the late 1970s. Remarkably, however, the Centurion continued in active service with the South African Defence Force up until 2003, over 60 years since it was originally designed.

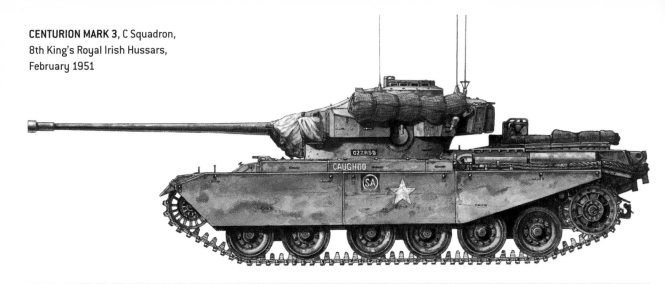

CENTURION MARK 3, C Squadron,
8th King's Royal Irish Hussars,
February 1951

SPECIFICATIONS

Crew: 4

Weight: 44.4 tonnes (49 tons)

Length: Hull: 7.56m (24.8ft), Gun forward: 9.8m (32.2ft)

Width: 3.37m (11.1ft)

Track width: 61cm (2ft)

Ground pressure: 12.8lb per sq.in.

Ground clearance: 50.8cm (1ft 8in)

Vertical obstacle climbing: 91cm (3ft)

Engine: Rolls-Royce Meteor Mark 4B

Transmission: Merritt-Brown Z51R

Fuel capacity: 550 litres (121 gallons)

Max. speed: 34km/h (21mph)

Main armament: ordnance QF 20-pdr (83.4mm) Tk Mk I

Secondary Armament: 7.62mm Browning MG

Rounds of ammunition: 65 20-pdr; 3,600 7.62mm

TANK DETAILS

Previous page: The first Centurion tank to fire in anger, commanded by Captain George Strachan MC, at Yongdungpo in Korea, 11 February 1951. The white star on the side of the tank was the original United Nations recognition symbol. The tank is liberally stowed with tarpaulins, bedrolls and crew comforts to ward off the bitter cold of the Korean winter.

This page: The Centurion last saw action with the British Army during the Gulf War in 1991. As part of Operation *Granby*, some Centurion AVREs (Armoured Vehicles Royal Engineers) were despatched to the Gulf, 40 years to the month since the Centurion's first operational deployment in the Korean War. Their role was to assault and breach the Iraqi main defensive lines. In the event, armoured engineer assistance was not needed but the fact that it was up-armoured for the role is clearly visible. Armour plates from the Warrior Infantry Fighting Vehicle have been added to the crew compartment and ERA blocks protect the turret.

CENTURION MARK V AVRE, 32nd Armoured Engineer Regiment, Operation *Desert Sabre*, Southern Iraq, February 1991

THE M26/M46 PERSHING TANK

The M26 Pershing was the ancestor of America's Cold War main battle tanks, the Patton tank series. The Pershing was designed during World War II, however, and was intended to counter the heavier German tanks, which the M4 Sherman was inadequate to deal with. The Pershing was received with enthusiasm, since it offered substantially better armour and firepower than the M4 Sherman medium tank.

One of the lingering controversies about the Pershing is why it was not put into service sooner. The standard US Army tank of 1944, the M4 Sherman medium tank, was clearly inadequate when facing newer German tanks such as the Panther, and the Pershing would have put the US Army on a more equal footing with the Wehrmacht in 1944. However, it did not enter service until after the great tank battles in Normandy and the Ardennes, and even then in very small numbers. US armoured doctrine maintained that the primary purpose of tanks was exploitation, not the engagement of enemy armour – this was to be done by specialized tank destroyers. This concept was subsequently shown to be unsound, but it played a part in delaying the development of a heavy US tank.

In 1948 an improved version of the M26, the M26E2, was renamed the M46 Patton, after General George S. Patton. Although intended for operations in Western Europe in World War II, the M26 and M46 tanks saw most of their combat in Korea. They proved highly effective against the NKPA's T34/85s, which had terrorized ROK forces early in the war, who had no effective counter to them as their existing armoured forces consisted mainly of M24 Chaffee light tanks. After the early, mobile stages of the Korean War, however, the fighting was mostly static and tanks saw limited use. They were still used to provide direct-fire support, but frequent mechanical problems began to sour the opinion of its crews. Nevertheless, the new design had proven itself against the excellent Soviet tanks, and the Patton series would go on to be used by the US Army until the 1980s with the introduction of the M1 Abrams.

T26E3 PERSHING, Co. B, 19th Tank Battalion, 9th Armored Division, Remagen, Germany, March 1945

SPECIFICATIONS

Crew: 5

Combat weight: 41.8 tonnes (46.1 tons)

Power-to-weight ratio: 10.8hp/ton

Overall length: 8.6m (28.2ft)

Width: 3.5m (11.5ft)

Height: 2.8m (9.2ft)

Engine: Ford GAF 8-cylinder liquid-cooled, 4-cycle gasoline engine

Transmission: torquematic with three forward, one reverse gears

Fuel capacity: 1,741 litres (383 gallons)

Max. speed (road): 48km/h (30mph)

Max. speed (cross-country): 32km/h (20mph)

Max. range: 160km (100 miles)

Fuel consumption: 5.1 litres/km (1.8 gallons/mile) (cruising)

Ground clearance: 43.7mm (1.7in)

Armament: M3 90mm gun in M67 mount

Main-gun ammunition: 70 rounds (M82 APC, T30E16 HVAP, T33 APBC-T, M71 HE)

Muzzle velocity: 808m/sec (2,650ft/sec) (M82)

Penetration: 120mm at 30 degrees at 500yds (M82 APC); 221mm at 30 degrees at 500yds (T30E16 HVAP)

Max. effective range: 19km (12 miles)

Gun depression/elevation: -10 / +20 degrees

Armour: 115mm gun mantlet; 76mm turret sides; 100mm hull upper front/76mm hull lower front; 50–75mm hull sides

TANK DETAILS

Previous page: Early Pershing tanks were very simply marked when they first went into combat. Aside from the normal Allied white stars on the turret side, glacis plate and engine deck, markings were confined mostly to shipping stencils painted on the side skirts. Note the large muzzle brake on the tank's M3 90mm gun.

This page: The M46 had a more powerful and reliable engine than the M26, enabling it to operate more effectively in the mountainous

terrain of the Korean Peninsula. This tank has an 18in-diameter searchlight mounted above the main gun, which was a recent innovation in 1952 to assist in night fighting. This tank has no commander's machine gun, probably because by this stage in the war tanks were generally used only for long-range fire support.

M46 PATTON,
Co. C, Marine 1st Tank
Battalion, Korea, 1952

THE T-54 AND T-55 MAIN BATTLE TANKS

The T-54 and T-55 family of tanks are the most important tanks of the post-World War II period, if only because of the sheer number manufactured. Over the second half of the 20th century they were widely exported to nearly all regions of the globe and have become almost as ubiquitous as the Kalashnikov assault rifle. Beginning with the invasion of Hungary in 1956, the T-54 and its derivatives have seen combat in nearly every major conflict.

The T-54 arose from the earlier T-44, which was developed in order to produce a tank superior to the most dangerous nemesis of World War II, the German Panther tank. The T-44's main drawback was its small turret, which was incapable of mounting anything larger than an 85mm gun. The T-54 had a larger turret and a 100mm gun. The first T-54 prototype was produced in 1945. It was accepted for service in April 1946 and entered production in 1947. The T-55 development could operate on a nuclear battlefield and was produced from August 1963.

The T-54 first saw action in 1956 during Operation *Vikhr* ('Whirlwind'), the action to crush the Hungarian anti-communist uprising. A number of T-54s were lost in combat, mainly to Molotov cocktails and Hungarian anti-tank guns. By the standards of the 1950s though, the T-54 was an excellent tank, combining lethal firepower, excellent armour protection and good reliability in a tank that was lighter and smaller than comparable Western designs such as the British Centurion or the American M48 Patton.

Since the end of the Cold War, former Warsaw Pact countries have sold off their obsolete tanks rather than scrap them, so now nations around the world employ the T-54 and T-55 as a cheap and effective main battle tank. Even though the T-54 and T-55 are outdated when facing state-of-the-art tanks, they are still a viable weapon in many regions, where they are often the most formidable weapon on the battlefield. The story of the T-54 and T-55 is far from finished.

T-54M, Syrian 5th Infantry Division,
Ramtha, Jordan, 1970

SPECIFICATIONS

Crew: 4

Combat weight: 35.9 tonnes (39 tons)

Power-to-weight ratio: 16.1hp/ton

Overall length: 9m (29.5ft)

Width: 3.27m (10.7ft)

Engine: V-55V 580hp (427kW) liquid-cooled V-12
diesel

Fuel consumption: 1.92 litres/km (0.67
gallons/mile)

Transmission: synchronized constant mesh with
planetary final drives, five forward, one reverse
gears

Fuel capacity: 960 litres (211 gallons) integral,
plus two 200-litre (44-gallon) external drums

Max. speed (road): 50km/h (31mph)

Max. speed (cross-country): 30km/h (18mph)

Max. range: 700km (435 miles) (with external
drums)

Armament: 100mm D-10T2S rifled gun

Main-gun ammunition: 43 rounds, typically:

6 x UBR-412 HEAT; 9 x 3UBM6 HVAP; 28 x UOF-
412 HE-Frag

Muzzle velocity: HE-Frag and HEAT: 900m/sec
(2,953ft/sec); HVAP: >1,000m/sec; AP-T:
1,000m/sec (3,281ft/sec)

Max. effective range: 1,500m (4,921ft)
(probability of hit >50 per cent)

Gun depression/elevation: -5 / +18 degrees

Armour: 205mm (turret front); 120mm
(turret side); 60mm (turret rear);
100mm (glacis plate and lower bow);
80mm (hull side) 50mm (hull rear)

TANK DETAILS

Previous page: Syrian armour took part in the fighting in Jordan in 1970, supporting the Palestine Liberation Organization against the Royal Jordanian Army. The Syrian 5th Infantry Division, reinforced with two armoured brigades and totalling nearly 300 T-54 and T-55 tanks, fought a savage battle with Centurion tanks of the 40th Armoured Brigade, losing 62 tanks in the process.

This page: This is a good example of how far evolution of the T-55 has progressed. The TR-85M1 upgrade adds a new gun, a rear turret bustle, appliqué armour,

new fire controls and host of other features. The colour scheme is indicative of Romania's interest in joining NATO, being a local variation of the current NATO three-tone scheme of dark green, chocolate brown and black.

TR-85M1, Romanian Army, 2000

THE M551 SHERIDAN TANK

The birth of airborne forces in World War II led to the first serious attempts to develop light tanks suitable for air-delivery in order to provide fire support for paratroopers. The US Army developed its first airborne tanks during the war, such as the M22 Locust, but the lack of a convenient means of delivery severely limited their deployment. With the advent of more substantial transport aircraft during the Cold War, however, further efforts were made to develop airborne armoured vehicles. The most ambitious of these programmes was the M551 Sheridan, which incorporated a variety of new technologies including a futuristic hybrid gun/missile armament. It was the most powerful light tank ever fielded, but it had a trouble-plagued career due to its over-ambitious armament.

Production of the Sheridan started in July 1966, and it entered service in June 1967 with 1st Battalion, 63rd Armor Regiment. The tank was first deployed in combat in Vietnam, where its light weight and technological immaturity undermined its combat effectiveness. Commanders felt that it was too vulnerable to mines and anti-tank rockets, which would often destroy the tank outright.

The most controversial feature of the Sheridan was its unusual main armament, a 152mm gun that could fire conventional rounds and the MGM-51 Shillelagh anti-tank guided missile. This was an attempt to give the light tank the power to engage more heavily armoured targets whilst remaining flexible. This weapon system was dogged by technical issues, including misfires and barrel damage, and it had a huge amount of recoil when firing conventional rounds, often lifting half the tank off the ground.

Although widely utilized in the armoured-cavalry role in Europe in the 1970s, the Sheridan's recurring technical problems led to its hasty retirement after only a decade. It remained in service with the 82nd Airborne Division, and was the first tank ever parachuted into combat, during Operation *Just Cause* in 1989. It saw combat again in Iraq in 1991, the only time when the Shillelagh guided missile was fired in anger.

SPECIFICATIONS

Crew: 4

Weight (combat loaded): 15.2 tonnes (16.8 tons)

Length: 6.27m (20.6ft)

Width: 2.8m (9.2ft)

Height: 2.9m (9.5ft)

Max. speed (road): 71km/h (44mph)

Max. range: 600km (375 miles)

Engine: Detroit Diesel 6V53T 300hp

Transmission: Allison XTG-250-1A with multiple wet plate, mechanical brakes

Suspension: independent torsion bar

Main gun: M81E1 152mm gun/launcher

Main-gun ammunition: 29 rounds (typically 10 missiles, 19 HEAT)

Missile armament: tube-launched, 152mm MGM-51 Shillelagh IR command-guided missile

Gunner's sights: M127A1 telescope, AN/VSG-2 Tank Thermal Sight

Secondary armament: co-axial M240 7.62mm; .50-cal M2 heavy machine gun on pintle

Chemical protection: individual crew masks connected to central filter

Armour: frontal protection against 50.-cal heavy machine gun

TANK DETAILS

Previous page: The Sheridan saw combat use in Vietnam, where it was found that it was better suited to operating on poor terrain than its heavier cousin, the M48A3. Despite this, it proved highly vulnerable and suffered high crew casualties. This tank has reactive armour blocks on the turret as protection against RPGs. The Sheridan's cramped turret led to crew fatigue, and many crews preferred to 'ride shotgun' outside the turret rather than risk being trapped inside the vehicle.

This page: The Sheridan was dropped by parachute during Operation *Just Cause*, the US invasion of Panama in 1989. By this stage the tank had acquired a number of modifications and upgrades, including the armoured screens around the commander's turret hatch known as the 'bird cage'. Note also the smoke-grenade launchers on the turret front and the storage bustle at the rear.

M55A1 SHERIDAN, Co. C, 3/73rd Armor, Operation *Just Cause*, Panama, December 1989

THE T-62 MAIN BATTLE TANK

The T-62 was developed out of the T-54/55 Soviet tank programme as a means of countering the new generation of NATO tanks such as the M60 that were coming into service. Armed with a radical new gun, it became the standard Soviet tank of the period, and was also widely exported throughout the world, particularly in the Middle East where it has had much of its operational experience.

The T-62 mounted a new design of gun, a 115mm smoothbore firing an APDS round. This gun required a larger turret and turret ring than that on the T-54/55, and so the chassis was lengthened, but otherwise many of the technical features were the same for the sake of economy. Although originally intended as a stopgap design, this new tank, accepted by the Soviet Army in August 1961, was to be the main Soviet medium tank for the following decade. The T-62 was first publicly displayed during the May Day parade of 1965 in Red Square, Moscow, and first came to widespread attention when some T-62 regiments were used in Operation *Danube*, the crushing of the reform movement in Czechoslovakia in 1968.

Although the T-62 was not widely used by other Warsaw Pact countries it was exported throughout the world, notably to Egypt, Syria and Iraq. It has seen extensive service in the wars in the Middle East during the second half of the 20th century, particularly in the Yom Kippur War of 1973, with Israeli tankers believing that the T-62 had the technological edge over their own upgraded Centurions, though their superior training proved decisive in the conflict. The Russians themselves used the T-62 extensively during their commitment in Afghanistan between 1979 and 1988, often dug in around firebases or used for convoy protection and infantry support. In more recent years the T-62 formed a significant part of the Iraqi tank force, and it was decisively outclassed by the modern NATO main battle tanks that confronted it.

T-62 MODEL 1962, Soviet 20th Guards Army,
Operation *Danube*, Prague, August 1968

SPECIFICATIONS

Crew: 4

Combat weight: 37.5 tonnes (41.3 tons)

Overall length: 9.33m (30.6ft)

Hull length: 6.63m (21.8ft)

Width: 3.3m (10.8ft)

Engine: V-55 580hp diesel with synchronized,

constant mesh transmission; planetary final
drives, five forward, one reverse gears

Fuel capacity: 675 litres (148 gallons) integral,
plus two 200-litre (44-gallon) external drums

Max. speed: 50km/h (31mph)

Max. range: 450km (280 miles); 650km (404
miles) with two 200-litre external drums

Main-gun ammunition: 40 rounds, (14 APFSDS,
20 HE-Frag, 6 HEAT)

Armament: U5-TS (2a20) 115mm smoothbore
gun with Meteor 2-axis stabilizers; -5 / +18
degree stabilization

Co-axial machine gun: 7.62mm PKT; 2,500
rounds of stowed ammunition

Turret armour: 230mm (front); 120mm (side);
60mm (rear); 30mm (top)

Hull armour: 100mm (upper glacis at 60
degrees); 80mm (side); 45mm (rear)

T-62 MODEL 1972, 3/6th Armoured Brigade,
3rd Saladin Armoured Division, Operation
Desert Storm, February 1991

TANK DETAILS

Previous page: The first significant operation employing the T-62 was Operation *Danube*, the invasion of Czechoslovakia in 1968. The tank shown here is in the standard Soviet green colouring, while the white bands are an air-recognition marking that dated back to the last days of World War II.

This page: Although largely replaced by the T-72 in elite units, the T-62 formed a significant part of the Iraqi arsenal in 1991, and saw a lot of combat in the Kuwait sector against M60A1 tanks of the US Marine Corps. Although these were also elderly models, the Marines' superior training and ammunition ensured their superiority and not a single M60A1 was penetrated by enemy fire.

THE IS HEAVY TANK

The IS (Iosef Stalin) series of tanks was born out of a growing sense of dissatisfaction within the Red Army about the performance of the KV series of heavy tanks. The KV lacked mobility and only mounted the same gun as the T-34, while the appearance of the German Tiger tank in late 1942 added a degree of urgency to the quest for a new heavy tank.

The first model in the IS series, the IS-1, was developed out of a modernization of the KV series, the KV-1S, with the hull being mated with a new turret armed with an 85mm gun. This was a short-lived design and it is unsure whether any were actually issued to combat units, as most were eventually upgraded to IS-2 standard. The IS-2 shared the same chassis as the IS-1 but mounted a different turret, this time equipped with a 122mm gun capable of penetrating the armour of the new German Tiger and Panther tanks. This tank went into production and the first examples became available to operational units in February 1944, when they were grouped together into separate Guards heavy tank regiments.

These units were used as 'breakthrough' forces, designed to spearhead Russian armoured attacks through heavily fortified German defensive positions. The first units went into action in April 1944 and proved extremely useful during Operation *Bagration* in the summer, before leading the attacks on the German capital of Berlin in April 1945. Further developments in the IS series resulted in the IS-3 with a completely redesigned turret offering significantly higher levels of protection, though this tank did not appear in time to see active service in World War II. Further variants were produced up to the IS-10, renamed T-10 following Stalin's death, before production of all Soviet heavy tanks was cancelled by Khruschev in 1960. The IS-2 and IS-3 saw widespread use outside the Soviet Union, being used by many Warsaw Pact countries as well as China and Egypt.

IS-2 MODEL 1944, 10-4th Tank
Regiment, 7th Guards Novgorodskiy
Tank Brigade, Berlin, May 1945

SPECIFICATIONS

Crew: 4

Combat weight: 41.7 tonnes (46 tons)

Power-to-weight ratio: 11.3hp/ton

Overall length: 9.91m (32.5ft)

Width: 3.07m (10.1ft)

Engine: V-2IS 4-stroke, V-type, 520hp diesel

Fuel capacity: 623 litres (137 gallons) internal,
363 litres (80 gallons) external, 500 litres
(110 gallons) supplementary

Transmission: multiple dry main clutch,
mechanical gearbox with reduction gear,
2-stage planetary turning mechanism and
side drives, eight forward, two reverse gears

Max. speed (road): 37km/h (23mph)

Max. speed (cross-country): 29km/h (18mph)

Max. range: 241km (150 miles)

Fording capability: 1.3m (4.3ft)

Muzzle velocity: 780m/sec (2,560ft/sec)

Armament: D-25T Model 1943 122mm rifled tank
gun

Fuel consumption: 2.25 litres/km
(0.8 gallons/mile)

Stowed main gun rounds: 28 rounds

Gun depression/elevation: -3 / +20 degrees

Secondary armament: DshK Model 1938 12.7mm
machine gun, co-axial DT 7.62mm machine
gun, DT 7.62mm close defence machine gun

Armour: 90–120mm (hull front); 90–95mm
(hull sides); 60mm (hull rear); (hull rear);
160mm (turret front); 100mm (turret rear
sides) 90mm (turret rear)

TANK DETAILS

Previous page: This IS-2 is painted in the standard Soviet scheme of dark green. It also has a white cross on the turret roof and bands around the turret sides to aid recognition from the air. As Soviet forces were advancing into Germany in 1945 they carried these markings to avoid any possible confusion by Anglo-American fighter-bombers.

This page: Egypt was one of the major foreign users of the IS-3, and 73 of them were lost in combat with the Israelis during the Six Day War of 1967, while there was at least one regiment still in service during the Yom Kippur War of 1973. This particular example is marked extravagantly as it was frequently used for parades in Cairo.

**IS-3M, EGYPTIAN 4TH ARMOURED
DIVISION,** Cairo, 1967

THE LEOPARD 1 MAIN BATTLE TANK

The Leopard 1 was the first indigenous German tank developed in the post-war period and proved the mainstay of the Bundeswehr Panzer units during most of the Cold War, as well as equipping the armoured forces of a number of NATO allies.

When the Bundeswehr was founded in 1955 its armoured units were equipped with US-made M47 and M48 tanks, which were increasingly obsolete in the face of Soviet developments in weapons technology. The German Government therefore decided to construct a MBT suitable for operations against the Warsaw Pact. Initially this was a project in cooperation with the French, but in the end the two countries undertook separate tank development, with the German project ending up as the Leopard 1 and the French as the AMX-30.

The Leopard 1 mounted the British L7A3 rifled gun, alongside a co-axial machine gun, while another machine gun was mounted on the turret for air defence. The initial versions of the Leopard 1 were quite lightly armoured compared to equivalent Soviet vehicles, as the designers believed that mobility and firepower were the key features of an MBT in an environment where hollow-charge weapons were supposed to dominate. However, subsequent variants have seen the armour protection level increased through a redesigned turret and appliqué armour to improve the survivability of the vehicle.

The tank was adopted for service in 1965 with the Bundeswehr, and also exported to a number of other NATO allies including Canada, Denmark and Belgium. Although the Leopard 1 has never seen action in German service, Danish Leopard 1s took part in peacekeeping operations during the war in Bosnia and engaged Serbian T-55s and self-propelled guns in 1994. The Leopard 1 has also seen active service with Canadian forces in Kosovo in 1999, as well as in Afghanistan as recently as 2006. To a large extent the Leopard 1 has now been replaced by the Leopard 2 in most NATO armies, though versions still exist as armoured recovery vehicles (ARVs) and bridgelayers.

LEOPARD 1A5, 2nd Co., Pz. Bn. 14, l. Pz. Grenadier
Bde., FTX 'Scharfer Bohrer', March 1990

SPECIFICATIONS

Crew: 4

Combat weight: 0.042 tonnes (0.046 tons)

Ground pressure: 14.0 N/cm²

Power-to-weight ratio: 19.7 PS/t

Hull length: 7.09m (23.3ft)

Overall length: 9.54m (31.3ft)

Width: 3.37m (11.1ft)

Height to turret roof: 2.61m (8.6ft)

Turning radius: 4.96m (16.3ft)

Engine: MTU MB 838 CaM 500, liquid-cooled V-90 37.4 litre four-stroke 10-cylinder multi-fuel engine developing 610 kW (830 PS) at 2,200rpm

Transmission: ZF4 HP250 planetary-gear shift with hydraulic torque converter; four forward, two reverse gears

Fuel capacity: 985 litres (216 gallons)

Max. speed: 62km/h (38.5mph)

Min. speed: 4km/h (2.5mph)

Max. speed reverse gear: 24km/h (14.9mph)

Fording capability: 1.2m (3.9ft)

Fording capability: 2.25m (7.4ft)

Underwater drive: 4m (13.1ft)

Slope: 60 per cent gradient, 30 per cent side slope

Main gun: 105mm riflebore L7A3

Stowed main gun rounds: 55

Gun depression/elevation: -9 / +20 degrees

Secondary armament: one co-axial MG 3, one air-defence MG 3

Smoke dischargers: eight Wegmann 76mm smoke mortars

LEOPARD C-1, A-SQD., VIII Canadian Hussars,
4th CMBG, Bergen-Hohne

TANK DETAILS

Previous page: This Leopard 1A5 belongs to the fourth batch produced for the Bundeswehr, built in 1970, and is shown in the three-colour FTA scheme that was later adopted by other NATO countries, including the US.

This page: This plate shows a Canadian Leopard C1 (very similar to German Leopard 1A3) as it would have appeared on the ranges at Bergen-Hohne in 1990. Although the Canadian forces were withdrawn from Germany in 1993, their Leopard tanks saw active service later in both Kosovo and Afghanistan.

THE M60 MAIN BATTLE TANK

The development of the M60 tank began in 1956 when the US Army sought to improve the design of the M48 tank and standardize the equipment issued to armoured units. Up until this point tank battalions had been equipped with an array of different tanks, and this wide variety of armour caused a logistical nightmare when it came to replacement parts and repair. Army strategists were also concerned about the new Soviet T-54, which looked like it would outclass all existing US tank designs. It was decided to use the M48 as the basis for all upgraded vehicles to meet the new threat, and modifying an existing model would save time and simplify logistical support.

A 105mm gun was fitted to the new tank, which was able to penetrate the armour of the T-54, as well as that of any other contemporary tank. The turret was not made larger, however, as it was felt that this would give the M60 too high a profile and make it a larger target. A bore evacuator was incorporated into the gun's barrel, which trapped gases within the barrel when the gun was fired, preventing them from being sucked back into the turret and affecting crew performance.

The M60 has seen battle in conflicts around the world for the last several decades, including the 1973 Yom Kippur War and Operation *Desert Storm* in 1991. The battle of the Golan Heights in 1973 drew much interest from US military planners, and it was found that the M60 could fend off significantly larger numbers of Soviet tanks. Weaknesses also became apparent, including the need for more armour in order to resist shoulder-fired anti-tank rockets. This sped up the development of appliqué bolt-on armour technology. In the invasion of Kuwait, the M60 proved itself capable of fighting against the Soviet T-55s, T-62s and T-72s it was designed to combat.

Today the M60 is still in use in many countries, despite the age of its design. Israel continues to use the M60, and Brazil, Spain, Turkey and Greece all have extensive numbers, along with several other nations.

M60 PRODUCTION MODEL

SPECIFICATIONS

Combat weight: 52.6 tonnes (58 tons)

Power-to-weight ratio: 14.24hp/metric ton

Ground pressure: 0.87kg/cm²

Hull length: 6.95m (22.8ft)

Overall length: 9.44m (31ft)

Width: 3.63m (11.9ft)

Height: 3.27m (10.7ft)

Length of track on ground: 4.24m (13.9ft)

Track width: 711mm (28in)

Ground clearance: 457mm (18in)

Engine: Continental AVDS-1790-2C 1790 Cubic Inch (29.34 litres), air-cooled V-12 stroke multi-fuel engine with 750hp at 2,400rpm

Final drive: Allison CD-850-6/6A powershift cross-drive transmission two forward, one reverse speed

Suspension: 6 road wheels per side with 3 return rollers. Road wheels mounted to torsion bars via idler arms

Max. speed (road): 48km/h (30mph)

Max. speed (cross-country): 16km/h (10mph)

Max. range: 480km (298 miles)

Fuel capacity: 1,420 litres (312 gallons)

Obstacle clearing, vertical: 91cm (3ft)

Obstacle clearing, trench: 2.59m (8.5ft)

Fording capability (unprepared): 1.22m (4ft)

Fording capability with fording kit installed: 2.4m (7.9ft)

Gradient climbing: 60 per cent

Main armament: 105mm M68 rifled gun with vertical breechblock

Secondary armament: co-axial 7.62mm M240 machine gun; 12.7mm M85 machine gun on commander's cupola

Ammunition stowage: 63 rounds (main gun), 900 rounds (co-axial and commander's machine guns)

TANK DETAILS

Previous page: The M60 was placed into production in 1960, with the first units being assigned to front-line troops mainly in Europe. This tank follows the standard colour and marking practice for the US Army in the 1960s, being painted in semi-gloss olive drab with flat white national insignia carried on the turret. Note the enclosed commander's cupola, which provided increased protection for this highly vulnerable crew member. Vision slots allow 360-degree visibility.

This page: This Armored Vehicle Launched Bridge (AVLB) is an M60 tank that has had the turret removed and replaced with a folding bridge and emplacement mechanism. The AVLB allows the installation of a bridge capable of crossing an 18m (60ft) gap while under hostile fire. Originally fielded in the 1960s, the AVLB continues to serve with US Army Engineer units.

Armored Vehicle
Launched Bridge

THE CHIEFTAIN MAIN BATTLE TANK

The Chieftain was the dominant main battle tank of the British Army during the Cold War, coming into service in 1967 and remaining in use until the 1990s, seeing active service in the Gulf War of 1991. It had been clear from the second half of 1944 that the British Army required a 'universal' tank, one that bridged the gap between the infantry and cruiser classes that all British tanks fell into. In the immediate post-war period the British relied on the last cruiser tank, the Centurion, and the heavy Conqueror and when it was time to replace them the requirement was for a single tank to fill both roles. The Chieftain, as it became known, developed out of this programme and was armed with the excellent L11 120mm high-velocity rifled gun, which had a unique two-piece ammunition system, with the charge being supplied in a combustible propellant case and thus removing the need for conventional brass cases. Other innovations on the tank included a reclining driving position, which meant that the tank could have a low profile. Five marks of the Chieftain were built, over 1,000 vehicles of which were used by the British Army, and it was also exported to the Middle East with Iran, Kuwait and Oman all taking quantities.

It was in the Middle East that the Chieftain was to see all of its operational experience. First, it was used extensively by Iran during the Iran–Iraq War of 1980–88. The Kuwaiti Army also used the Chieftain, and 18 managed to escape across the Saudi border following the Iraqi invasion in August 1990. Refurbished by the British, these tanks re-entered Kuwait during Operation *Desert Storm* in February 1991. Although the British Army did not deploy Chieftain tanks to the Gulf (the Challenger 1 was used instead), ARRVs (Armoured Repair and Recovery Vehicle) and AVREs (Armoured Vehicle Royal Engineers) based on the Chieftain were taken in order to support the armoured forces. The Chieftain remained in British service until 1995 and is still in service in Iran.

CHIEFTAIN MARK 2(Y) C, 5th Royal Iniskilling Dragoon Guards
Battlegroup, Exercise Medicine Man, BATUS, Canada, July 1970

SPECIFICATIONS

Crew: 4

Combat weight: 55 tonnes (60 tons)

Length (gun forward): 10.58m (34.7ft)

Width: 3.7m (12.1ft)

Height: 2.9m (9.5ft)

Ground clearance: 51cm (20in)

Ground pressure: 88.3KN/m²

Road speed: 48km/h (30mph)

Vertical obstacle: 0.9m (3ft)

Max. gradient: 60 degrees

Trench-crossing capability: 3.15m (10ft)

Fording capability: 1.07m (3.5ft)

Engine: Leyland L60, liquid-cooled, compression ignition, 26.11 capacity

Output: 720bhp at 2,100rpm

Transmission: TN12 Merritt-Wilson with six forward and two reverse gears

Suspension: Horstmann with 12 pairs of twin wheels in six bogies.

Main armament: OBL 120mm L11A3 rifled tank gun with fume extractor and thermal sleeve

Ammunition: 64 rounds of 120mm, 6,800 rounds of 7.62mm and 600 of .50-cal

Secondary armament: L8A1 7.62mm co-axial machine gun and L37A1 7.62mm machine gun on commander's cupola, plus .50-cal ranging gun

CHIEFTAIN MARK 2(Y) L, Headquarters Squadron, The Queen's Royal Irish Hussars, Paderborn, BAOR, 1978

TANK DETAILS

Previous page: A Chieftain in the camouflage pattern commonly used at BATUS, the extensive British Army training facility located in Alberta, Canada. Covering 2,500km², this facility allows for large-scale exercises that would be impossible given the space limitations of MOD facilities in the UK.

This page: This Chieftain sports the dark-green and black temperate-zone camouflage pattern used throughout the British Army in the 1970s and 80s. This particular vehicle is shown on the ranges in Paderborn; the green flag indicates that it is not loaded with live ammunition.

THE T-72 MAIN BATTLE TANK

The Russian T-72 Ural tank is one of the most widely deployed main battle tanks of recent generations. It was used not only by the armies of the former Warsaw Pact and Soviet Union, but it has been exported in large numbers to many states in the Middle East. It has seen combat in many recent conflicts, including the 1982 invasion of Lebanon, the Iran–Iraq War, the Chechen Wars and both the 1991 and 2003 Gulf Wars.

Initial production of the Obiekt 172 tank began in 1972 at Nizhni Tagil. The early service trials of the Obiekt 172 regiments led to an immediate improvement programme to rectify flaws in the design, under the codename 'Obiekt 172M'. This model became the first of the series produced in large numbers, designated the T-72. Production began in 1974 and was initially earmarked exclusively for Soviet Army use.

The T-72's crew compartment is extremely cramped, even compared to earlier Soviet tanks such as the T-62; American and European main battle tanks are luxurious by comparison. Neither the commander nor gunner can stand in the turret with the hatches closed since the autoloader cassette in the hull floor takes up so much space. The use of an autoloader rather than a human loader supposedly gives the main gun a higher rate of fire, but in practice tank engagements depend upon the first vital moments of contact, where a well-trained M1 Abrams crew can get off three rounds in 15 seconds, which would be impossible with the T-72 autoloader's invariable reload time of eight seconds.

In the Gulf War, the T-72's poor fire-control system was its primary failing. The Iraqi crews often found it impossible to engage the Americans due to poor weather conditions, and even when engagements did take place at short ranges, the T-72 was completely outclassed. The reinforced armour of the M1A1HA Abrams could withstand 125mm fire from the frontal quadrant, which is believed to have occurred on seven occasions. Conversely, the T-72s had inadequate armour protection to resist the heavier Western tanks, such as the Abrams and Challenger, it faced in Kuwait and Iraq.

SPECIFICATIONS

Crew: 3

Combat weight: 37.1 tonnes (41 tons)

Power-to-weight ratio: 19.8 hp/ton

Hull length: 6.86m (22.5ft)

Overall length: 9.53m (31.3ft)

Width: 4.75m (15.6ft) (with side skirts), 3.59m (11.8ft) (side skirts removed)

Height to turret roof: 2.19m (7.2ft)

Engine: V-46-6 12-cylinder, four-stroke, multi-fuel diesel, 780hp (575kW) at 2,000rpm

Transmission: mechanical, synchromesh, seven forward, one reverse gears

Fuel capacity: 1,000 litres (220 gallons) integral, +400 litres (88 gallons) external

Max. speed (road): 60.6km/h (37.3mph)

Max. speed (cross-country): 45km/h (28mph)

Best cruising speed: 40km/h (25mph)

Max. range: 483km (300 miles) on internal fuel

EAST GERMAN T-72M, 4th Bn., MSR Renner, 9th Panzer Division, Drogeheide, DDR, 1990

Fuel consumption: 2.8 litres/km (1 gallon/mile)

Fording capability: 1.2m (3.9ft) (without preparation), 5m (16ft) (with preparation)

Slope: 30 degree gradient, 25 degree side slope

Obstacle: 0.85m (2.8ft) vertical, 2.9m (9.5ft) trench

Main gun: 2A46M (D-81TM) 125mm smoothbore

Muzzle velocity: 1,800m/sec (5,900ft/sec) (3UM7 APFSDS); 850m/sec (2,790ft/sec) (30f19 HE-Frag)

Max. effective range: 2km (1.2 miles)

Stowed main gun rounds: 44

Gun depression/elevation: -6 / +14 degrees

Secondary armament: co-axial PKT 7.62mm machine gun

Smoke dischargers: Type 902A; 12 cover 300m^2 for two minutes

Crew self-defence: AK-74S assault rifle, 10 F-1 grenades

IRAQI T-72M, 2nd Regiment, 12th Armoured
Brigade, 3rd Saladin Armoured Division,
Kuwait, 1991

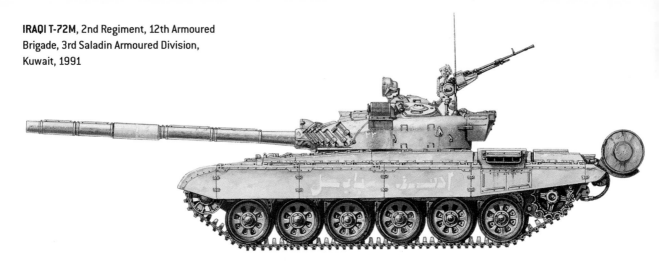

TANK DETAILS

Previous page: The T-72's small size reflects its design as an offensive weapon, sacrificing armour protection for increased speed and mobility. It also presents the enemy with a smaller target to fire at. This East German tank has been camouflaged in the usual medium-green colour, which was lighter than standard Warsaw Pact or Soviet green, with sprayed bands of light grey and charcoal black.

This page: This late-production T-72M with smoke mortars is finished in an overall dull sand colour. Note the prominent external fuel drums at the rear and the small turret. A 12.7mm NSVT 'Utes' anti-aircraft machine gun is mounted on the commander's cupola.

THE MERKAVA MAIN BATTLE TANK

The Merkava is the first ever Israeli-produced main battle tank. Work began in 1971, and the project was dubbed the 'Chariot Programme'. Unlike Western tanks, designed for use on the plains of Europe, Israel needed a desert-warfare vehicle that could operate on the rough terrain of the mountainous north of Israel and desert hills in the east.

The primary concern was crew protection; armament and mobility would have to come second. Throughout the design process, the Israeli Defense Force (IDF) was conscious of the devastating tank losses they had taken in the 1973 Yom Kippur War, and was determined to find remedies to prevent such loss in future conflicts. To facilitate this, the Merkava incorporates several unusual features for a modern tank. The driver is placed in the crew compartment, removing a long-existent psychological isolation. The engine is at the front of the tank, not at the back as is conventional, which provides the crew with additional protection from frontal hits. There is a rear escape hatch, which also enables a few infantrymen to travel with the tank, or to keep a casualty comfortable until he can be removed to an aid station. It can also be used to resupply ammunition quickly and easily. The hull and turret's low profile and sloped armour decrease the angular impact of incoming projectiles, and enables a hull-down position to be achieved more easily.

The new tank's baptism of fire came on 6 June 1982, when tens of thousands of IDF troopers crossed Israel's northern border with Labanon to initiate Operation *Peace for Galilee*. In the pitched and sometimes desperate battles of Sultan Ya'aqub and Ein Zehalta, the Merkava defeated everything the Syrians threw at it – armour, infantry and anti-tank helicopter gunships.

The latest design variant, the Merkava IV, was introduced in 2004 and is optimized for urban combat. It was used in the 2006 Lebanon War, where it proved vulnerable to anti-tank missiles and IEDs, though the IDF has attributed this to poor tactics, not the design of the tank itself. The Merkava was also used in the 2008 Gaza conflict.

MERKAVA MARK I, 77th Bn., 7th
Armored Bde., Jerusalem, 1979

SPECIFICATIONS

Crew: 4

Combat weight: 63 tonnes (69 tons)

Length (gun forward): 8.3m (27.2ft)

Length (hull): 7.45m (24.4ft)

Width: 3.7m (12.1ft)

Height to turret roof: 2.64m (8.7ft)

Height to commander's cupola: 2.75m (9.1ft)

Ground clearance: 47cm (18.5in)

Power-to-weight ratio: 15hp/ton

Engine: Teledyne Continental AVDS-1790-6A V12
diesel 900hp

Transmission: General Motor CD-850-6BX
semi-automatic

Suspension: 1st generation

Trench-crossing capability: 3m (9.8ft)

Fuel capacity: 900 litres (198 gallons)

Max. speed: 46km/h (28.5mph)

Armour protection: classified

Max. range: classified

Armament: L7/M68 105mm gun

Ammunition: classified

Secondary armament: 2 FN MAG 7.62mm light
machine guns; 60mm mortar; optional gun
mount .50-cal heavy machine gun; optional
Mk.19 40mm grenade launcher

Ammunition capacity: 62 rounds/ 105mm;
10,000 rounds/ 7.62mm; 2,500 rounds
of .50cal

TANK DETAILS

Previous page: When the IDF first unveiled the Merkava to a crowd of dignitaries and Armored Corps veterans, the impact of this new vision of steel and ballistic firepower was overwhelming. This tank is adorned in the 'out-of-the-factory' greyish-sand scheme, belonging to the 7th Armored Brigade's 77th 'Oz' ('Courage') Battalion.

This page: While resembling its two predecessors, the differences between them and the Mark III are considerable, none more obvious than the modular-type armour applied throughout the tank. The Mark III follows the same 'Chariot' design and has the same battlefield accessories as its predecessors.

MERKAVA MARK III, 188th 'Barak'
Armored Bde., Northern Israel, 1990

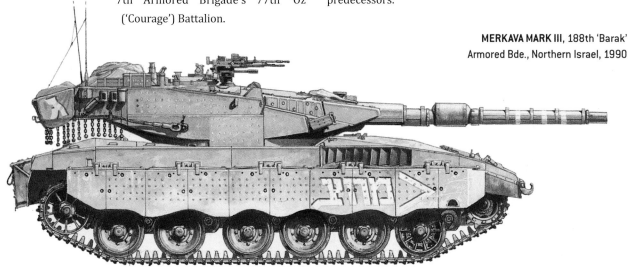

THE CHALLENGER 1 MAIN BATTLE TANK

The Challenger 1 provided the backbone of the regiments of the British Royal Armoured Corps throughout the 1980s and early 1990s until its replacement by the Challenger 2. Its origins lay in a 1974 order for an improved version of the Chieftain MBT by the Imperial Iranian Army. This order was cancelled following the fall of the Shah's regime in 1979 and, combined with the cancellation of the British MBT-80 project due to cost overrun, led to the adoption of an upgraded version of the new tank by the British Army, now renamed the Challenger.

The first operational tanks entered service with the British Army in 1983, and its distinguishing features – and main advantages over its predecessor the Chieftain – were in the areas of protection and mobility. The Challenger was the first British tank to use the revolutionary Chobham armour, which is a composite structure of ceramic and metal that gives vastly increased protection against hollow-charge warheads, which make up the vast majority of anti-tank weapons. The new hydrogas suspension system, along with an improved powerpack, ensured that the Challenger had much greater reliability and cross-country mobility than its predecessor. The principal drawback to the Challenger as a tank design was its fire-control system, which compared unfavourably with other NATO MBTs of the period.

Despite this, the Challenger performed well under combat conditions when it was called on during the first Gulf War of 1990–91 and Operation *Desert Sabre*. The upgraded Challenger 1 units of the 1st (UK) Armoured Division, including the 'Desert Rats' of 7th Armoured Brigade, proved markedly superior to their Iraqi opponents, with the TOGS (Thermal Observation and Gunnery System) of the Challenger allowing the British units to acquire and eliminate their adversaries before they could come into range. The Challenger proved to be a highly reliable tank in the desert, and destroyed over 300 AFVs without a single Challenger being lost to enemy action.

CHALLENGER 1 MARK 3, D SQN.,
The Royal Scots Dragoon Guards
(Carabiniers and Greys), 7th
Armoured Bde. Group, Saudi
Arabia, 14 November 1990

SPECIFICATIONS

Crew: 4

Combat weight: c.60 tonnes (66 tons)

Length (gun forward): 11.55m (37.9ft)

Width: 3.52m (11.5ft)

Height to commander's cupola: 2.88m (9.4ft)

Ground clearance: 50cm (20in)

Ground pressure: 0.9kg/cm²

Road speed: 60km/h (37mph)

Vertical obstacle: 0.9m (2.9ft)

Max. gradient: 30 degrees

Trench-crossing capability: 3.15m (10.3ft)

Fording capability: 1.07m (3.5ft)

Engine: Perkins Condor 12-cylinder 60 V direct injection 4 stroke diesel, compression-ignition

Fuel capacity: 6.1 litres (1.3 gallons), rating 1,200 BHP (859kW) at 2,300 rpm (BSS), 11,296 BHP (DIN)

Generator: 500 amp

Transmission: TN37 epicyclic – four forward gears, three reverse gears, automatic transmission with torque converter

Suspension: hydrogas type

Main armament: ordnance breech-loading 120mm tank gun L11A5

Ammunition: minimum of 44 projectiles consisting of APDS, HESH, SH/Practice, DS/T Smoke, 42 charge containers each holding one APDS or two HESH rounds

Secondary armament: 7.62mm TKL8A2

TANK DETAILS

Previous page: The 7th Armoured Brigade of Western Desert fame was one of the major units operating Challenger MBTs during the first Gulf War of 1990–91. These Challengers used in the desert were comprehensively upgraded on arrival in the desert through the use of 'Challenger improvement kits', designed to improve reliability and survivability. Such was the success of this upgrade that 174 out of 176 Challengers committed to the ground campaign were fit to cross the start line in February 1991.

This page: Operation *Desert Sabre* was not the only time that the Challenger 1 was used operationally; it also saw service as part of the British commitment to UN and NATO operations in the former Yugoslavia. Shown here is a Challenger 1 Mark 3 of the Queen's Royal Hussars operating as part of IFOR, the NATO Implementation Force inserted to see that the terms of the Dayton peace agreement were being kept to by all sides.

CHALLENGER 1 MARK 3, B Sqn., The Queen's Royal Hussars, IFOR, Operation *Resolute*, Central Bosnia, 11 January 1996

THE LEOPARD 2 MAIN BATTLE TANK

In spite of its name, the Leopard 2 is not simply a new version of the well-known Leopard 1. On 11 December 1974 a Memorandum of Understanding was signed between the Federal Republic of Germany and the US, for the possible joint production of a new tank. The Leopard 2 entered production in 1979, and it is now the main battle tank of the German Army.

Its layout is conventional, with the engine at the rear and driver in the front right and the commander, gunner and loader in the turret. Both the commander and loader's hatches have ring mounts for 7.62mm machine guns for air defence, though the weapon is normally fitted to the loader's hatch. The Rheinmetall 120mm smoothbore main gun was the most powerful tank gun available when the Leopard 2 entered service in 1979. It can fire both kinetic and HEAT rounds, enabling it to engage different targets with a degree of flexibility. The Leopard 2 also has excellent mobility, with a maximum road speed of 68km/h (42mph) (though it is limited to 50km/h [31mph] in peacetime) and the ability to drive underwater through a depth of 4m (13ft) when a snorkel is fitted beforehand.

The Leopard 2 has been used by Germany in Kosovo and by Canada and Denmark in Afghanistan. In general the Leopard 2 has been found to be very durable when hit by improvised explosive devices (IEDs), though at least one crewman has died as a result of IED explosions in Afghanistan. NATO commanders have praised its effectiveness in battling the Taliban, where its well-balanced combination of firepower, mobility and protection enables it to lay down powerful fire from a secure armoured platform and operate in the rugged terrain of Afghanistan.

The Leopard 2 is currently in service with the armies of Austria, Denmark, Germany, the Netherlands, Norway, Switzerland, Sweden and Spain. The German Army plans to keep it in service until approximately 2030, which would make the Leopard 2 one of the longest-serving tank designs in history.

LEOPARD 2 A4 (SECOND BATCH), 4th Company, Panzerbataillon
24, 1. Panzer-Division, Braunschweig, 1991

SPECIFICATIONS

Crew: 4

Combat weight: 55 tonnes (60.6 tons)

Ground pressure: 8.3N/cm²

Power-to-weight ratio: 27PS/t

Length (hull): 7.72m (25.3ft)

Length (overall): 9.67m (31.7ft)

Width: 3.75m (12.3ft)

Height to turret roof: 2.48m (8.1ft); 2.87m
(9.4ft) to top of PERI-R 17

Turning radius: 9.5m (31.2ft) (turret at 6
o'clock); 11.5m (37.7ft) (turret at 12 o'clock)

NBC protection system: Dräger-Piller compact
system, working on up to 4 mbar overpressure

Engine: MTU MB 873 Ka-501, liquid-cooled V-12
47.6-litre 4-stroke exhaust turbo-charged
diesel engine, developing 1,500 PS (1,104kW)
at 2,600rpm

Transmission: Renk HSWL 354 hydro-kinetic
planetary gear shift, four forward and two
reverse gears

Max. speed (road): 68km/h (42mph)

Max. speed in 2nd reverse gear: 31km/h
(19mph)

Fuel capacity: approx. 1,160 litres (255 gallons)

Fording capability: 1.2m (3.9ft)

Underwater drive depth: 4m (13.1ft)

Slope: 60 degree gradient, 30 degree side slope

Obstacle: 1.1m (3.6ft) vertical, 3m (9.8ft) trench

Main gun: Rheinmetall 120mm L/44 smoothbore

Stowed main-gun ammunition: 42 rounds

Gun depression/elevation: -9 / +20 degrees

Secondary armament: one co-axial 7.62mm MG 3
A1, one air-defence 7.62mm MG 3 A1

Smoke dischargers: 16 Wegman 76mm smoke
mortars, firing DM 35 smoke mortars either
in single rounds or in groups of four, with the
ability to also fire fragmentation grenades

TANK DETAILS

Previous page: The tank shown here is an upgraded vehicle with the ammunition-supply hatch welded shut to enable better NBC (nuclear, biological, chemical) protection. This Leopard 2 A4 has the standard camouflage scheme and tactical markings applied, and has an anti-aircraft-defence machine gun attached to the loader's turret hatch.

This page: Later-production Leopard 2s have sloped armour at the front of the turret, replacing the blocky design of earlier tanks and increasing the likelihood that incoming projectiles will be deflected away. This tank is painted in the standard camouflage scheme adopted in 1984 of green, brown and black. This German-developed scheme was later adopted in a similar form by many other nations, including the US, which used it for its M1A1s delivered in 1986.

LEOPARD 2 A5 (FORMER SIXTH BATCH),
Panzertruppenschule, Münster, 1996

THE T-80 MAIN BATTLE TANK

The T-80 tank was meant to be the ultimate Soviet MBT, entering the Soviet arsenal around the same time as the new NATO-generation American M1 Abrams, British Challenger and German Leopard 2. In the event, the T-80 proved to be deeply troubled, offering modest advances over the existing T-64A and T-72 tanks, yet being considerably more expensive due to the use of a gas-turbine engine. At the time of its design in 1976 it cost R480,000 versus R143,000 for the T-64A.

The main advantage of the T-80's gas-turbine engine is that it offers a very high power output from a relatively small and lightweight engine, giving the tank exceptional speed and mobility. Its most serious drawback is its ferocious appetite for fuel, consuming an average of 240kg/hour compared to 83kg/hour for a comparable diesel engine.

Production of the original T-80 design was short lived, running from 1976–78; the total number produced was probably well under 200 tanks. The improved T-80B design was accepted in 1978 and became the most common production version of the T-80. The tank has evolved continuously since then, with the T-80U having explosive reactive armour bricks, smoke-grenade launchers and armoured side skirts. The T-80UD and T-80UM have diesel engines rather than the gas-turbine engine.

The T-80's performance in the Chechen conflict in the 1990s was poor. Unfamiliar with the voracious appetite of the tank's gas-turbine engine, crews left the engines running, not realizing that the tank consumed as much fuel at idle as it did when running. During the assault on the Chechen capital, Grozny, in December 1994, tanks were hastily ordered into the city without adequate tactical planning, resulting in 70 per cent losses. Whilst the tank's frontal armour was good, RPG hits against the vulnerable engine deck could easily penetrate to the ammunition, causing a chain of catastrophic explosions. The debacle caused controversy in Moscow, and in 1996 the Russian Army announced that the T-90 would be the preferred tank for the immediate future. Nevertheless, the T-80 was the backbone of Russian tank forces by the late 1990s.

T-80B, Leningrad Military
District, 1989

SPECIFICATIONS

Type: T-80BV (Obiekt 219RV)

Crew: 3

Weight (loaded): 39.6 tonnes (43.7 tons)

Overall length: 9.65m (31.7ft)

Width: 3.58m (11.7ft)

Height: 2.21m (7.3ft)

Clearance: 45cm (17.7in)

Engine: GTD-1000TF gas-turbine; 1,100hp

Fuel stowage: 1,840 litres (404 gallons)

Power-to-weight ratio: 25.17hp/ton

Max. speed: 70km/h (43mph)

Range: 335–370km (208–229 miles)

Turret armour: cast steel armour shell, cavity with
ceramic rods in front quadrants,
Kontakt-1 ERA

Hull armour: rolled steel plate with glass-
reinforced plastic laminate in glacis plate

Main gun: 125mm 2A46M-1 Rapira-3 smoothbore,
6–8rpm

Ammunition stowage: 38 main gun rounds

Missile capability: 9K112-1 Kobra radio-guided,
tube-fired missile with 9S461-1 fire-control
system

Anti-aircraft MG: 12.7mm NSVT (300 rounds)

Co-axial MG: 7.62mm PKT (1,250 rounds)

Fire-control system: 1A33 with 1G42
sight/range-finder and 1V517 ballistic
computer

Gunner's night sight: TPN-3-49 image
intensification

Commander's sight: TKN-3V day/night sight

Gun stabilizer: 2E26M

Radio: R-123M transceiver; R-124 intercom

T-80UD (OBIEKT 478BE), Al-Zarar,
41 Horse, 1 Armoured Division,
Pakistan Army, 2005

TANK DETAILS

Previous page: The T-80B was the first T-80 tank produced in large numbers, and was the first version to be forward deployed with the Group of Soviet Forces in Germany (GSFG) starting in 1981. The tank's turret is small and cramped, containing the commander, gunner and an autoloader in place of a third crewman.

This page: This T-80UD has a 1,100hp diesel engine instead of the thirsty gas-turbine engine found in most other variants. Explosive reactive armour can be clearly seen on the turret front. This is designed to defeat HEAT warheads by blasting the shaped-charge explosions away from the tank's armour, thereby limiting its penetrative effectiveness.

THE CHALLENGER 2 MAIN BATTLE TANK

The Challenger 2 is the current MBT operated by the armoured regiments of the British Army; it has been in service since 1998 and it is expected to remain in use until 2035. The development of the tank originated in a private design by Vickers Defence Limited as an upgrade to the original Challenger 1. Following perceived limitations in the fire-control and turret designs of the both the Chieftain and the Challenger 1, the British Government decided to replace the Chieftain with a new MBT in 1987. Following an unusually open procurement procedure, with the US M1A1, German Leopard 2 and French Leclerc all being considered, the contract for the new tank was awarded to Vickers for the newly named Challenger 2.

Although the Challenger 2 shared its name and chassis structure with its predecessor, the two vehicles only had about 5 per cent of components in common, with the turret of the Challenger 2 being a completely new design incorporating a new L3 120mm rifled gun as well as an upgraded fire-control system.

The Challenger 2 has seen extensive operational service since its acceptance by the British Army in 1998. In 2000 a squadron was deployed to Kosovo as part of KFOR, NATO Kosovo Force. The tanks were used as a deterrent force to keep apart the warring factions through the use of road patrols and fixed vehicle checkpoints. More traditional tank-versus-tank combat was seen when Challenger 2s participated in Operation *Telic*, the British involvement in the 2003 invasion of Iraq. Once again the Challengers formed part of the 7th Armoured Brigade, 1st (UK) Armoured Division, and had been upgraded for desert conditions based on their experiences on exercise in Oman in 2001. Some 120 Challenger 2s were used during the course of the operation, and proved as effective at dealing with the Soviet-era Iraqi armour as its predecessor the Challenger 1 had been, with once again no losses from enemy fire.

CHALLENGER 2, B SQN., The Royal Scots Dragoon Guards (Carabiniers and Greys), Operation *Agricola III*, Kosovo, May 2000

SPECIFICATIONS

Crew: 4

Combat weight: 62.5 tonnes (68 tons)

Length (gun forward): 11.5m (37.7ft)

Width: 3.52m (11.5ft)

Height: 2.49m (8.2ft)

Ground clearance: 50cm (19.9in)

Ground pressure: 0.9kg/cm²

Road speed: 59km/h (36mph)

Vertical obstacle: 0.9m (3ft)

Max. gradient: 60 per cent

Trench-crossing capability: 2.34m (7.7ft)

Fording capability: 1.07m (3.5ft)

Fuel capacity: 1,592 litres (350 gallons)

Engine: Perkins Engines Company CV12 TCA V-12 12-cylinder turbo-charged aspiration air-to-air charge cooling 26.1 litre diesel

Model: No. 3 Mark 6A

Output: 1,200bhp at 2,300rpm

Transmission: David Brown Defence Equipment Ltd TN54 epicyclic transmission with six forward and two reverse gears

Steering: commercial hydraulics double differential hydrostatic control

Suspension: hydrogas

Secondary armament: William Cook double-pin track

Main armament: 120mm L30A1 rifled gun

Secondary armament: co-axial 7.62mm L94A1 chain gun and roof-mounted 7.62mm L37A2 machine gun

TANK DETAILS

Previous page: The British involvement in Kosovo, Operation *Agricola III*, in 2000 saw the first operational deployment of the Challenger 2 MBT. This particular tank of the Royal Scots Dragoon Guards is equipped with both passive and reactive appliqué armour panels, an operational upgrade set known as Dorchester Level 2.

This page: Although initial ground operations in Iraq were over quite quickly after the invasion of March 2003, the British deployment in Iraq continued for many years afterwards and this plate depicts a Challenger 2 of the 4 Royal Dragoon Guards in 2004. Desert camouflage is no longer used and the Dorchester Level 2F appliqué armour is used for increased survivability against IEDs and RPGs.

CHALLENGER 2, A SQN., The Royal Dragoon
Guards, Operation *Telic*, Majar-al-Kabir, Southern
Iraq, 28 December 2004

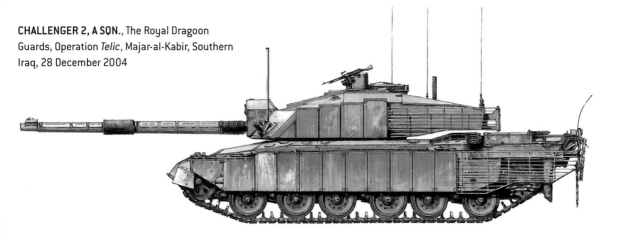

THE M1 ABRAMS TANK

The M1 Abrams tank is the most radical departure in US tank design since World War II. Until the early 1980s, the US Army had relied on the steady evolution of the M26 Pershing tank: the M46, M47, M48 and M60. The M1 was the culmination of programmes begun in the 1960s to replace the M60 series. Its design came at a time when there was a host of important new tank technologies coming to fruition: special armours, thermal-imaging sights, advanced gun fire controls and gas-turbine engines. These were all integrated into the M1 tank design.

The M1 Abrams was first committed to combat in 1991 during Operation *Desert Storm*. During the war, the M1A1 Abrams was credited with destroying over 2,000 Iraqi tanks, with not a single Abrams being destroyed by hostile tank fire. The fighting highlighted the Abrams' advanced optical equipment, which enabled crews to engage targets through dust and poor weather as well as at night. Being able to acquire and fire at their target first (and at ranges of over 3,500m – over 2 miles) ensured that the Americans fought at a considerable advantage. The depleted-uranium sabot round used was nicknamed the 'silver bullet', as it proved extremely effective at piercing enemy tank armour.

The Abrams' own survivability is increased by internal ammunition compartmentalization inside a large turret bustle, which prevents catastrophic ammunition fires inside the turret. Blast doors fitted to the turret roof are designed to direct internal fires and explosions upwards, away from the crew.

The Abrams was used effectively during the 2003 invasion of Iraq. The success of the Abrams design has led to a slowing down of MBT design in recent years, as there has been little incentive for America to develop a more effective tank design. The M1A1 and improved derivatives like the M1A2 have ensured that the Abrams remains one of the world's best tanks, and it is unlikely that it will be replaced for many decades.

M1A1 ABRAMS, A Co., 1-37 Armor,
1st Armored Division, KTO,
January 1991

SPECIFICATIONS

Crew: 4

Combat weight: 56.7 tonnes (62.6 tons)

Power-to-weight ratio: 24 hp/ton

Hull length: 7.9m (26ft)

Overall length: 9.8m (32.2ft)

Width: 3.6m (11.8ft) (with side skirts), 3.4m
(11.2ft) (side skirts removed)

Engine: Textron Lycoming AGT 1500 gas turbine,
1500hp

Transmission: Allison X1100-3B hydrokinetic,
four forward two reverse gears

Fuel capacity: 1,909 litres (420 gallons)

Max. speed (road): 67km/h (41.7mph)

Max. speed (cross-country): 48km/h (30mph)

Best cruising speed: 40km/h (25mph)

Max. range: 442km (275 miles) (cruising speed)

Fuel consumption: 5.16 litres/km
(1.83 gallons/mile)

Fording capability: 1.2m (3.9ft)

Armament: M256 120mm cannon

Max. effective range: 3,500m (APFSDS), 3,000m
(HEAT-MP)

Main-gun ammunition: M829 APFDS (Armour-
Piercing, Fin-stabilized, Discarding Sabot);
M830 HEAT-MP (high-explosive, anti-tank,
multi-purpose)

Muzzle velocity: 1,676m/sec (5,500ft/sec)
(APFSDS), 1,138m/sec (3,735ft/sec)
(HEAT-MP)

Gun depression/elevation: - 10 / + 20 degrees

M1A1, I Tp, 3 Armd. Cav. Regt., KTO, January 1991

TANK DETAILS

Previous page: Appropriately enough, the 37th Armor traces its lineage back to the 37th Tank Battalion, commanded by Creighton Abrams in World War II. Several special markings were adopted in the battalion, including a cartoon on the bore evacuator, a shark in this case. The machine gun has been covered up to prevent it from being fouled by sand and dust.

This page: This Abrams, named *Road Beast*, is equipped with a mine plough, designed to scoop up anti-tank mines and push them aside. Note the machine-gun cover to keep out sand and dust, and the stowage around the turret. The Abrams' large turret contains an ammunition bustle at the rear, separating it from the crew behind an armoured blast door.